MW01076534

Cyprus CUISINE

christina loucas

Editor and proofreader Patrick Geraghty
Design Tanya Montini

Library and Archives Canada Cataloguing in Publication
Title: Cyprus cuisine / Christina Loucas.
Other titles: Cucina di Afrodite. English
Names: Loucas, Christina, author.
Description: Translation of: La cucina di Afrodite. | Includes index.
Identifiers: Canadiana 20200415786 | ISBN 9781770503373 (softcover)
Subjects: LCSH: Cooking, Cypriot. | LCGFT: Cookbooks.
Classification: LCC TX725.C93 L6813 2021 | DDC 641.595693—dc23

Whitecap Books acknowledges the financial support of the Government of Canada through the Canada Book Fund (CBF)
for our publishing activities and the Province of British Columbia through the Book Publishing Tax Credit.

Printed in Hong Kong by Sheck Wah Tong Printing

whitecap

Cyprus CUISINE

christina loucas

whitecap

Dedication

I would like to dedicate this book to three people.

First, to my mom, Katherine Loucas. She has been the source of so many recipes and has helped me test and retest the recipes in here so many times I have lost track. She will always take time to help me out, gather ingredients and show me how to properly make things, even when I think I know it well enough myself. I have told her numerous times that this book is as much hers as it is mine. Anyone reading it should know. She features prominently in my Instagram account, so much so that people ask for her next appearance. She is a force in the kitchen, as so many Cypriot mothers are. This book is for you.

Second and third, to my family: my love Steven Doyle and my daughter Clementine (Clemmie). To my sweets for your incredible support and advice and superb recipe-tasting skills (!) while writing the English version of this cookbook. You always made it easy for me, and gave me the support I needed to see this project through to the end, which means so much to me and was no easy task, especially during the first six weeks of raising a newborn! Also, I had no idea that when I was snapping pictures of clementines two years ago, long before publication of the English edition of this book, I would give birth to a daughter named Clementine. Alas, she is not named after the fruit, but I think it is one of life's special coincidences that one of my favourite photographs from this book happens to be a plate full of citrus fruit, including clementines! The picture is hung in our kitchen, just outside her nursery.

I also just want to add that it seems appropriate to be dedicating this book to two generations of women in my family. Many of these recipes were handed down to me by my mother and my aunts, and I am sure that my mother and aunts learned these recipes the same way. I hope that one day Clementine might read this book and cook from it, and that it will serve as a wonderful reminder of her family's roots, and her mother's recipes too.

Table of Contents

Introduction

During my childhood, I would visit Cyprus every summer with my mom and sister. We would take a plane from Vancouver Island and fly across the world to land on a tiny island in the far eastern corner of the Mediterranean Sea, arriving in Cyprus in the middle of the night, where the plane doors would open and let in a blast of warm, salty, humid air. Later, we would take a taxi—usually a shared, cramped, old Mercedes—and travel along a windy mountain road at far-too-fast a speed, to end up in my grandma's mountain village, Amargeti.

Amargeti is a typical Cypriot mountain village— cactus pears grow along the road, grape vines swirl around your head. In the past, my grandma's homemade halloumi would hang from the corners of her house and old, unmarked glass bottles of homemade lemon squash would line the inside of her refrigerator, waiting to greet visitors. Olive and lemon trees always stood heavy with fruit, just as they probably had for hundreds of years.

As I grew up, family trips to Cyprus became sporadic, overtaken eventually by the hustle and stress of my work as an international arbitration lawyer in London, England. I noticed that each time I did manage to visit Cyprus there were less and less of the homemade foods I remembered from my childhood—no more halloumi homemade by my Grandma, who was now too old, and no more homemade orange blossom water, as my great-aunt had passed away. The older generation was literally dying off and taking their knowledge of how to make these traditional foods with them. Worse, when I looked for a cookbook telling me how to make these recipes, I could not find one that explained things in a way I could relate to. I realized that if I wanted to preserve my family's recipes, I would in fact have to figure out a way to do it myself.

Fast forward to February 2011. It was one o'clock in the morning on a snowy Monday night in London, England. I was still at work, as

we had a filing due the next day. I had ordered a cab, but because of the snow, it was taking hours to arrive. I fell asleep under my desk at Gray's Inn, and my secretary Debbie woke me up when it arrived. On the cab ride home, I started concocting an escape plan from my job, which—despite working for an incredible mentor, and on some of the world's most interesting international arbitration cases—I felt ready to take a break from. I started to imagine moving to Cyprus to write a cookbook to preserve the traditional recipes I thought were being forgotten. I never actually thought I would do it. Then, six months later, I flew to Cyprus.

I thought my trip would be a brief adventurous career break. My loving family supported my decision, but a lot of people were shocked. They said I would be "throwing away" my legal career and my Oxford University legal education, comments that made me feel bad. In the end, I wavered and took a position at a fantastic Cypriot law firm, albeit determined to "do the cookbook on the side." Unsurprisingly, I ended up working more than blogging, and before I knew it I began to find myself more and more physically exhausted. This time, however, the consequences were more dire.

As it turned out, the reason I was so tired was because I was actually sick. Suddenly, about one year after I had arrived in Cyprus, I was back in London, this time in the intensive care wing of London Bridge Hospital with serious complications from a thyroidectomy. I was surrounded by an incredibly caring hospital staff and my family, but it was a challenging time—I had intentionally stalled my career, my nine-year relationship had just crumbled, I had no thyroid and no voice and I was still to undergo iodine therapy. I spent the next two months at my aunt's house in Cyprus watching Columbo reruns with my neighbour and childhood friend Athos, waiting for my voice and my physical and mental strength to return.

After that experience, I felt like I had nothing to lose. I saw life anew. I began to put all my energy into my blog, and I started taking photography lessons for no other reason than purely because I was interested in doing so. I unapologetically followed my passions, and lived without guilt or fear. I enjoyed life. Which is how my blog, my food photography career and this book took its first steps—they are, in essence, my silver linings.

It seems fitting that I would begin to explore the culinary world in some form, having grown up in the restaurant business with a father who was a well-known restaurateur in British Columbia and a mother who was a trained baker. I was seating customers when I was two years old, and bussing tables when I was 11. The return to a project in the culinary realm has been comforting.

ABOUT CYPRIOT COOKING

This is a Cypriot cookbook. I have set out to capture the essence of traditional Cypriot cooking in a way that makes it accessible to a modern, international kitchen. This book is about preserving my favourite traditional recipes in a way that is approachable whether you are familiar with Cypriot food or not. It is also about sharing some modern Cypriot recipes that I believe showcase the traditional ingredients and flavours associated with Cyprus. I wrote this book with the same goals I had when I started my blog: to offer those living outside of Cyprus a glimpse into this small but distinct culinary world, as well as to keep Cyprus's culinary traditions—many of which I fear are being forgotten as the older generation passes away—alive for those who have enjoyed them all their lives through a visual and written story that will evoke memories of childhoods past.

Cyprus is a small island in the southeast Mediterranean Sea. The closest countries to it include Lebanon, Israel, Syria, Egypt, Turkey and Greece. The island has a rich history and has been influenced by many different cultures throughout the centuries including Greek, Roman, Ottoman and Venetian, all of which have played a role in shaping Cypriot cuisine.

There is sometimes a tendency to assume that Cypriot food is the same as Greek food. While there are similarities, certain methods and recipes are unique to Cyprus. Cyprus has a humble but alluring eastern Mediterranean cuisine where Mediterranean and Middle Eastern flavours and ingredients mix together. There are some recipes that are largely distinct to Cyprus itself, such as flaounes, and some recipes that are almost identical to ones found in Greece and Turkey, simply

4

with different names and small differences. For example, makaronia tou fournou, Cyprus' version of lasagna, is also made in Greece, but in Greece it is called pastitsio and is made with tomato sauce and beef, whereas in Cyprus it uses pork and leaves out the tomato. Likewise, in Cyprus, bulgur wheat is used to create a tomato pilaf called pourgouri and pork filled donuts called koupes. While similar dishes can be found in Turkish cuisine, I have found it to be harder to find these dishes made with bulgur wheat in Greek cuisine.

Traditional Cypriot cooking is, at its heart, a simple cuisine. Like many families, my grandparents came from small mountain villages—my mom's parents from Amargeti (near Paphos), and my dad's parents from Lapithos (near Kyrenia). Both of my grandparents were farmers who made use of the fresh seasonal Mediterranean vegetables and fruits they grew and foraged around them, of which there were many: grapes, olives, carobs, figs, oranges, mandarins, Seville oranges, lemons, bergamot, apricots, plums, peaches, pomelo, grapefruit, watermelon, cantaloupe, kumquats, cactus

pears, medlars, almonds, walnuts and more. Olive oil, olives and red wine vinegar were always on the kitchen table. Orange blossom water and rosewater could be found inside the cupboards. Cheeses like halloumi and Anari were made on a regular basis. Regular meals usually consisted of seasonal pulses served with no more than a drizzle of olive oil, a generous squeeze of lemon and a side of bread and marinated olives. In the mountain villages, seafood was not eaten often, as it was not easy to come by. In general, from the stories I have been told by my family, it was not an easy life.

Most Cypriot dishes are not particularly hot or spicy, although there is ample use of local herbs such as wild oregano, rosemary, mint, parsley, basil, cinnamon and coriander. Spices such as allspice, cloves, mastic and mahleb powder can be found in many sweets and baked goods.

Though Cyprus is a small country, there is quite a large variety of different dishes there. I think this can be attributed to the many different cultures that have influenced the island, as well as the fact that there is a big difference in climate around the country. One can be suntanning on the beach in Limassol, then one hour later be driving through snow-covered mountains. There are also differences in how the same recipes are made across the island, which is something I continue to discover. For example, I always thought that stuffed zucchini flowers were vegetarian, but in some villages of Cyprus they actually add meat. For such a small island, the cuisine can vary quite considerably.

To some extent, traditional Cypriot cuisine hasn't changed much since my grandparents' time. Simple, seasonal farm cuisine involving a variety of vegetables is still very popular today. Meat is enjoyed on a more regular basis, as well as during religious celebrations and at large family gatherings. Many families still make homemade olive oil every year, and friends and families still exchange excess bounties of homegrown fruits and vegetables with one another. Traditional pickled and foraged foods are enjoyed as much as they ever were, though more and more these foods are being produced or gathered by increasingly aging populations or else purchased at stores. Though fewer people have time to make bread or traditional homemade pastries, a plethora of bakeries now exist around the island, many of which are open 24 hours a day—a perk which I have always enjoyed!

I think it bears mentioning that—even though this is a cookbook—Cyprus is a country with complex political issues. While all of this is important in its own context, it's not something I choose to go into detail about here, apart from mentioning the fact that when I refer to Cypriot recipes, I am talking about Cypriot recipes as I have learned them from my family and friends, which happen to be Greek Cypriot recipes as opposed to Turkish Cypriot recipes.

THE RECIPES IN THIS BOOK

You will find both traditional and modern Cypriot recipes inside this book. Some are my family's traditional Cypriot recipes that I

wanted to preserve, and these I have left unchanged as I think alterations would defeat the purpose of preservation. However, I have provided modern methods for preparing recipes in cases where doing so does not affect the foods themselves, so that they can be made in any kitchen. Some are modern Cypriot recipes, where I have modernized traditional Cypriot recipes by incorporating Western ingredients or methods. Growing up in Canada and having lived in London, Singapore and Bangkok, it was difficult to find some traditional Cypriot ingredients, and I was forced to experiment by finding local substitutes. I soon learned that modifying recipes can actually be a good thing, and any traditional purism I held in my heart has disappeared over the years. Some of the mixed Cypriot recipes I make are actually more delicious (in my opinion) than the traditional ones. Conversely, over the years, I have also learned which Cypriot ingredients I simply cannot do without, and these I now always make room in my suitcase for no matter where I go. This is why you will find some "non-Cypriot" recipes that incorporate Cypriot ingredients and flavours.

Overall, this book is my personal selection of Cypriot recipes. My selection is by no means perfect, and it is definitely not exhaustive, but I have made an effort to include those recipes that have meaning to me. I am very much aware that each individual Cypriot family will have its own unique touch to each traditional recipe. So please do not think that my ingredients or methods are set in stone. There are many wonderful cooks and recipes in Cyprus.

RECIPE GUIDE

This is a book filled with both traditional and modern Cypriot recipes. I have provided Greek translations of titles for the traditional Cypriot recipes, but not for the modern Cypriot recipes. This way, the reader will be able to keep track of the Cypriot recipes versus the "non-Cypriot" recipes that simply incorporate Cypriot flavours and ingredients.

Cypriot recipes are fairly easy to make, although some can be time consuming. It is worth remembering that big family meals are still the norm in Cyprus, even in today's busy world. It is also not un-common to find one person in each family (perhaps a grandmother)

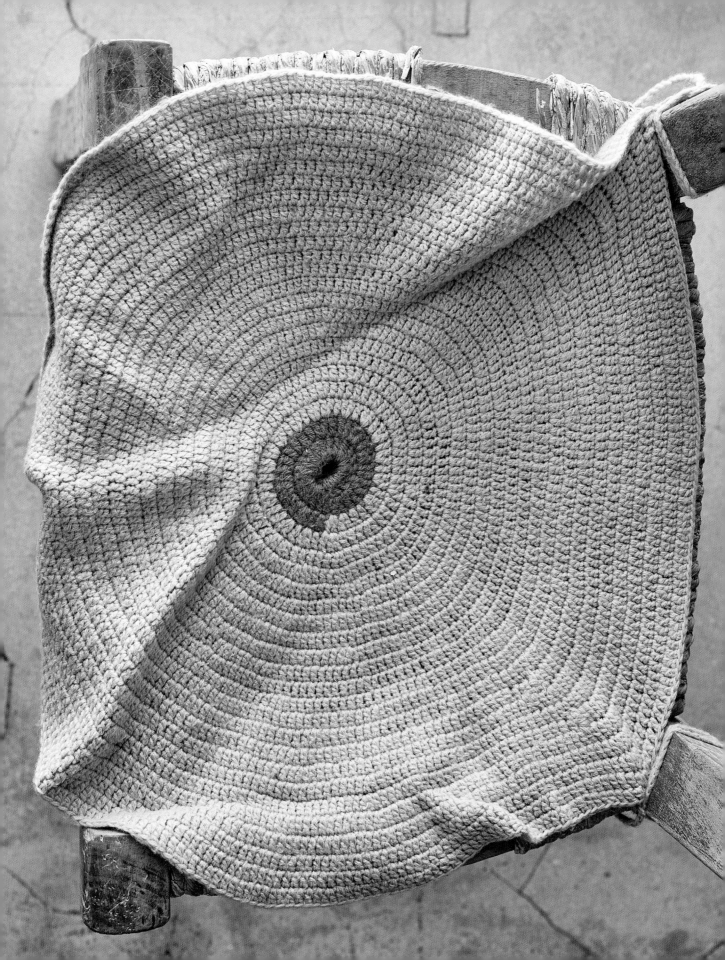

who continues to cook for their kids and grandkids. When baking sweets and cookies, the tendency is still to make a lot and give to ones' friends. I have tried to adjust quantities in this book so that the recipes are easily made for two people. But some of the recipes inside this book can still feed a crowd. For these, you can simply halve the recipes to make less.

I really think the type of kitchen equipment you choose to use is an individual choice. I have made do for many years simply with a handheld electric mixer and the usual pots and pans. I know that this is more than what my grandma had to work with, but I couldn't do without them. For the most part, you will not need any special equipment to make the recipes in this book. I have listed and described some of the specific kitchen equipment below.

As for the ingredients you will need, most should be easy to source from any large grocery store, and those that are more unique to Cyprus

you should be able to buy from any speciality Mediterranean or Middle Eastern shop. Where I think an ingredient may be difficult to source outside of Cyprus, I have included suggested substitutes.

There are also some recipes that call for very specific ingredients and kitchen equipment. These relate to traditional recipes that I have included largely for preservation and nostalgic purposes, rather than for reproduction, including the Orange Blossom Water on page 169, Soured Wheat Soup with Halloumi on page 101, Pickled Caper Shoots on page 171 and Grape Jelly on page 198. These specific recipes and methods are very old, and I have included them because I wanted to preserve the techniques and methods my family uses, as well as for interest's sake. It is not recommended that you attempt to make these recipes yourself, but I have included them because I feel it is nice to retain the method in which my family made these recipes. For example, I do not expect people to have fresh Seville orange blossoms and a distiller on hand, but wanted to explain the process of how certain recipes were made for anyone like me who remembers their yia-yias making such things and wanted to hold on to a memory of sorts.

In terms of measurements, I have used both volume and weight, whichever I think makes the process easier. In Cyprus, I have discovered that a "cup" does not seem to mean a measuring cup of international standards, but rather a random cup that every household seems to own! In this book, however, a cup holds 250 mL, a teaspoon holds 5 mL and a tablespoon holds 15 mL. All measurements are level unless otherwise specified. "Scant" means a little less than full, and "heaped" means a little more than full.

Finally, please bear in mind that in Cyprus there is quite a bit of humidity and heat. As a result, if you live in a cooler or drier climate, do not be put off if you need a little more or less flour for a dough to come together. If the dough looks too soft, do not be afraid to add more flour until it is pliable, or vice versa.

IMPORTANT INGREDIENTS AND TOOLS YOU WILL NEED

In the above section I touched on some of the ingredients and tools you might need in this cookbook. In this section, I list some specifics to provide you with a bit more information and background on the types of ingredients mentioned in certain recipes, as some of them may not be familiar to those new to Cypriot cooking. You should be able to find the below ingredients and tools at a Mediterranean or Middle Eastern grocery store, and I have tried to mention substitutes where possible in the individual recipes.

Cheeses

Halloumi: Halloumi is a type of traditional Cypriot cheese made with sheep and/or goat milk. Most versions that you buy in stores now also contain cow milk, but this isn't the traditional form. In any event, you can find halloumi in most major grocery stores now in North America. If you do see a brand that uses only sheep and/or goat milk I would recommend buying this.

Anari Cheese: Anari cheese is similar to a salty ricotta, and is a by-product of halloumi. It is extremely difficult to find Anari cheese outside of Cyprus, but luckily the Greek cheese Mizithra is very similar and is a great substitute. You can find Mizithra in most Mediterranean or Middle Eastern grocery stores.

Spices and Dry Ingredients

Mahleb or Mahalepi Powder: This is a spice used frequently in Greek, Cypriot and Middle Eastern baking that you will see pop up a few times in the bread section of this book. Mahleb powder is a spice with a flavour similar to bitter almond and cherry. It is made from the seeds of the St Lucie cherry. You have to be careful with it as it can sometimes add a bitter taste to your food if you use too much. I usually buy pre-ground mahleb powder, as it makes for easier baking.

Mastic Powder: Mastic is a resin derived from the mastic tree. Originally a sap, it dries into little pieces of dried resin, which are then ground to form mastic powder. You can chew the dried resin. It will first taste bitter, then release flavours similar to pine and cedar.

16

Mastic powder is used frequently in Greek, Cypriot and Middle Eastern baking. In this book, you will see it used in the bread section, but it is worth mentioning that in Cyprus it also used in ice cream and other delights. Again, be careful not to use too much, as it will make your food bitter. I usually buy pre-ground mastic powder as it makes for easier baking.

Vanilla Powder: I perfected many of the recipes using vanilla powder as opposed to vanilla extract, which we use more frequently in North America. However, if you cannot easily find vanilla powder or prefer to use vanilla extract, simply substitute ¼ tsp (1 mL) vanilla powder for 1 tsp (5 mL) vanilla extract. Also, ensure that you add the vanilla extract to the wet ingredients rather than the dry ingredients as you would with the vanilla powder.

Village Flour: This is essentially a yellow flour made from durum wheat that is high in protein. It is used to make a lot of Cypriot breads, pastries and pastas. Here, I recommend using bread flour as a substitute.

Syrups and Waters

Carob Syrup: Cyprus is covered in carob trees, and it was once a very valuable export. The term "carat" that used to measure the weight of precious stones and gold is derived from the practice of measuring gold against the weight of carob seeds. It is mostly thought of as a chocolate substitute, but I find this misleading. To me, the flavour is more akin to butterscotch and caramel. In fact, I like to think of carob syrup as the maple syrup of Cyprus. Growing up, we would slather it all over pancakes, and it makes a delicious dip for bread when mixed with tahini. You can find carob syrup in most health foods and specialty Mediterranean and Middle Eastern shops. Carob honey is likely to be more difficult to source, but regular honey can be a substitute in some situations (see p. 75).

Orange Blossom Water: Orange blossom water is used in many Cypriot desserts, and it adds a delightfully subtle and sweet floral taste to your food if used properly. It is easily found in specialty Mediterranean and Middle Eastern shops. I have also explained how to make it in this cookbook, but only for preservation purposes.

Tools

Handheld Milk Frother: In the frappe recipe (p. 35), you will need to buy a handheld battery-operated milk frother. I have always tried to find a substitute for this, but the truth is that a frappe just simply won't produce enough foam if you don't have one of these magical little whisks on hand. The good news is that you can find them in stores that sell coffee equipment, and I even bought mine from a store specializing in matcha tea products, as frothers are also used to prepare matcha tea.

Briki: This is the little pot in which Cypriot coffee is traditionally made. It will be needed if you wish to make Cypriot coffee. I have been able to source these from most kitchenware shops outside of Cyprus.

Drinks

Wherever you go in Cyprus, you can find people sitting and enjoying drinks together, whether a quick Cypriot coffee under a makeshift tent at the local market, coffee and a game of backgammon enjoyed by old men at a coffee shop, frappes by the beach or relatives drinking afternoon glasses of lemonade together on a veranda.

There are a few drinks that I think are ubiquitous throughout Cyprus, specifically Cypriot coffee and homemade lemonade. No matter where you are—a relative's home, a beach restaurant, a rural taverna—these items always seem to be on offer.

This section contains a few of my favourite drink recipes that I will always enjoy when I am in Cyprus.

CYPRIOT COFFEE (KYPRIAKO KAFE)
Κυπριακός Καφές

Very rarely will you not be offered a Cypriot coffee when visiting someone else's house in Cyprus. In the old parts of town and the farmers' markets it is still quite common to see people wandering around in the early morning carefully balancing large trays filled with Cypriot coffees alongside customary glasses of water. You would think that making Cypriot coffee is a fairly simple affair, but ask anyone who makes it what their "technique" is, and you will discover a new method each time. Traditionally, Cypriot coffee was made with a Cypriot coffee maker called a "briki" that is placed in hot sand in order to evenly heat the coffee while making it. Nowadays, instead of hot sand, a stove or little electric coffee maker is used. In my family, we still have a large collection of small-to-large brikis ready for any number of guests should they appear. Those who enjoy Cypriot coffee will have a preferred way of drinking it: unsweetened, semisweet or sweetened.

½ cup (125 mL) cold water
2 tsp (10 mL) Cypriot coffee
sugar, to taste
Cypriot coffee maker (briki)

Pour water and coffee into a Cypriot coffee maker (called a "briki"). Add 2 tsp (10 mL) sugar for very sweet (glyko), 1 tsp (5 mL) for sweet (metrio) or no sugar at all (sketo) and place the briki over high heat on a stove. Stir well until the coffee and any sugar have dissolved.

Before the coffee begins to boil it will create a rising foam on the surface of the coffee. When this occurs, immediately remove the briki from the stove, otherwise the coffee will burn and taste bitter and you will not be left with much foam. Hold the briki over a cup and pour the coffee. Serve with a glass of water.

Makes 1 coffee.

CYPRUS LEMONADE (LEMONADA)

Λεμονάδα

Homemade lemon squash is a drink that is always on hand in most Cypriot households—there is usually a bottle of homemade lemon squash made by a relative stored in an unmarked glass bottle in the fridge, awaiting guests. I am told by my aunt that the trick for good-quality Cypriot lemon squash is to make it using lemons that have just changed colour from green to yellow, and also to squeeze some of the oil from the lemon rind into the squash. The oil helps to make the lemon squash last longer in the fridge, as the oil will create a natural layer that stays on top of the lemon squash, protecting it from the air. Perhaps it also helps that Cypriot lemons are some of the most aromatic and enticing I have ever enjoyed.

3 cups (750 mL) freshly squeezed lemon juice (approx. 10 to 15 lemons)
3 cups (750 mL) sugar
ice cold water, for serving

Squeeze the lemons to obtain their juice. If you have an old-fashioned juice press where pressure is applied to the lemon peel, this is ideal as it will squeeze out some of the oil from the peel into the juice, causing the squash to last longer and taste better.

Pour the juice into a small bowl. Add the sugar, and stir together with a wooden spoon until the sugar has totally dissolved. Pour the lemon squash into a sterilized bottle and store in the fridge.

When serving, add ¼ cup (60 mL) lemon squash for every 1 cup (250 mL) ice cold water (more or less to your preferred sweetness).

Makes 12 servings.

LEMON VERBENA ICED TEA

Lemon verbena is an herb found around Cyprus that is traditionally dried and made into tea. It has a strong lemon scent. This lemon verbena iced tea is an exotic interpretation of Cypriot lemonade and iced tea. Though it is written as a non-alcoholic drink, my friends and I found that a touch of gin makes it a perfect afternoon cocktail on a hot day!

Heat and stir ½ cup (125 mL) water and sugar until the sugar has dissolved. Let cool, then add the juice of 1 lemon to the mixture. Add the lemon verbena leaves and English Breakfast tea bag (if using) to 6 cups (1.5 L) boiled water and let brew for 20 minutes.

In a large jug, add the lemongrass sticks, chopped ginger, fresh mint leaves and tea. Slice in the remaining lemon. Add the sugar mixture to the iced tea until sweetened to taste. Place in the fridge until cool, strain and serve with ice.

Makes 4 to 6 servings.

6 cups (1.5 L) + ½ cup (125 mL) water, divided
½ cup (125 mL) sugar
2 lemons, divided
1 cup (250 mL) fresh verbena leaves
1 English breakfast tea bag (optional)
4 crushed lemongrass sticks
½ cup (125 mL) chopped ginger
½ cup (125 mL) fresh mint leaves

MRS. NONA'S
CITRUS SPRITZER

Alexis' mom, Nona, makes the best citrus squash I have ever had. When you open the bottle, it really feels like you are smelling an orange grove. Listening to her explain to me how to make it made it abundantly clear why—her first instruction to me was to "gather the fruit," and even during this step there is a technique behind it!

2 ½ cups (625 mL) pressed mandarin juice
2 ½ cups (625 mL) pressed orange juice
5 cups (1.25 L) sugar
ice cold sparkling water, for serving

Use mature and sweet mandarins. If gathering them, gather them in the morning before the sun hits the fruit. When pressing the mandarins and oranges, try to use an old-fashioned press that also presses and releases the oil from the peels into the squash—this adds flavour and helps preserve the squash.

Stir the juices and the sugar in a bowl until the sugar has dissolved, then let the mixture rest for 2 hours before pouring the squash into a sterilized bottle and storing it in the fridge.

When serving, add ¼ cup (60 mL) orange squash for every 1 cup (250 mL) ice cold sparkling water (more or less to taste).

Makes 20 servings.

YIA-YIA'S ELDERFLOWER AND SAGE HERBAL TEA REMEDY

(ZAMBOUCOS AND SPAJIA)

Ζαμπούκος and Σπατζιά

This isn't so much a recipe, but I think it is important in a Cypriot cookbook to mention these teas as they still play a role in my family's kitchen as well as others in my aunt's village. Whenever I came down with a cold in Cyprus, my family would always make me one of these two soothing teas. One is made with dried wild sage leaves and a spoonful of honey, while the other is made with dried elderflower leaves and (again) a spoonful of honey. Both types of leaves were gathered from the village and stored in unmarked plastic containers in our kitchen cupboard. My relatives would always say that both of these teas were good for sore throats, and that the elderflower tea in particular was good for a cough. Even in Canada, these are still my go-to teas to make when I come down with a cold.

1 cup (250 mL) boiling water
2 to 3 sprigs of dried elderflower blossoms or 1 tsp (5 mL) dried sage leaves
1 tsp (5 mL) good-quality honey

Boil the water. Add the sprigs of dried elderflower blossoms or dried sage leaves to the water and let brew for 5 minutes. Stir in honey and enjoy.

Makes 1 serving.

FRAPPE (FRAPPE)

Φραπέ

When I asked my friend Alexi to give me a frappe recipe, he said to me "that's like asking me how to boil an egg." His point being that everyone in Cyprus knows how to make frappes—except, apparently, for me. During the entire time I lived in Cyprus I simply preferred to ask a friend or family member to make me a frappe. Greek coffee I could make no problem, but frappes always tasted better to me when someone else made them! I like to think of a frappe as a bit like a coffee shake. They are enjoyed all year round in Cyprus, but my favourite time of year to enjoy them is in the summertime by the beach. You can vary the sugar level as well as the milk level and, despite me not wanting to make them, they are truly very easy to make. In the end, I managed to twist Alexi's arm, and he kindly provided this recipe to me. Note that you will need a handheld milk frother for this recipe. I have tried other ways to make frappes, but this is truly the best and easiest way in my opinion, as other methods won't produce as much froth.

In a tall glass, add coffee granules and your desired amount of sugar. Add about 1 to 2 Tbsp (15 to 30 mL) water, enough to just cover the coffee granules and sugar. Using a handheld milk frother, blend the mixture until it appears frothy and solid. You should be able to turn the glass upside down and the froth should stay put.

Add ice cubes to the top of the glass, then fill the glass with water and/or milk depending on your preference.

Makes 1 frappe.

1 tsp (5 mL) instant coffee granules (the Nescafé brand is quite popular in Cyprus)

sugar, to taste (up to 2 tsp/10 mL)

1 to 2 Tbsp (15 to 30 mL) water (approx.)

ice cubes

milk, to taste (up to a nearly full glass)

Bread & Pastries

Bread and pastries play an important role in Cypriot food. In a country where most shops' opening hours can be somewhat limited, I think it speaks volumes that bakeries are one of the few commercial establishments that sometimes remain open 24 hours a day.

There are many breads and pastries in Cypriot cuisine. Because there are so many different types, I did not include them all. What I have included are the traditional bread and pastry recipes that my family still makes. There are also a number of newer pastry recipes I have included, which I enjoy by incorporating Cypriot flavours into Western classics, and which can easily be enjoyed outside of Cyprus.

EASTER ORANGE BREAD (TSOUREKI)

Τσουρέκι

This is a delicate, sweet, orange-scented braided bread that reminds me a bit of challah and is made at Easter in Cyprus. You can tell if it is a good tsoureki because you will see little threads when you tear open a piece. This characteristic is created because of the way the dough is kneaded. This bread also makes for fantastic French toast when it is too old to be enjoyed plain.

In a small bowl, stir together the yeast, milk and 1 tsp (5 mL) sugar. Cover the top of the bowl with plastic wrap and let rise for 10 minutes until frothy.

In another large bowl, mix together the dry ingredients. In a third bowl, beat the eggs and remaining sugar on high speed for 7 minutes.

Add the melted butter to the flour mixture with the orange juice, yeast mixture and egg mixture; mix together with your hands until a dough forms. Vigorously knead the dough for 10 minutes until it becomes smooth and elastic, using your thumbs to press the top of the dough downwards towards you then away from you—this will create the nice texture. Create a ball with the dough and place it in a bowl. Cover the bowl with plastic wrap and a couple tea towels. Let it rest for 2 hours, until it has doubled in size.

Divide the dough into 3 pieces, then divide each piece into a further 3 ropes and create 3 braids. Place on a baking tray. Cover the braids with a tea towel and let them rise for 1 ½ hours, until the dough has doubled in size.

Preheat oven to 325 °F (160 °C). Before placing the braids in the oven, brush with egg wash. Bake for 30 to 35 minutes.

Makes 3 braided loaves.

1 envelope yeast (8 g)

½ cup (125 mL) lukewarm milk

½ cup (125 mL) + 1 tsp (5 mL) sugar, divided

1 ¼ lb (550 g) all-purpose flour

¾ tsp (4 mL) mahleb powder

¼ tsp (1 mL) mastic powder

⅛ tsp (0.5 mL) vanilla powder

pinch of salt

3 eggs

½ cup (125 mL) melted butter

2 Tbsp (30 mL) fresh orange juice

½ Tbsp (7 mL) orange zest

1 egg, beaten for egg wash

OLIVE BREAD (ELIOPITA)
Ελιόπιτα

In Cyprus, there are many versions of olive bread. There is the traditional bread made in a large pan called a *sini*, there are individual semi-circular olive pies in a soft pastry crust and there are big rolls, all of which are sold in every bakery and food market. I love this version with a crusty sesame exterior and lots of filling on the inside. Most olive pies in Cyprus add fresh cilantro, but I feel it overpowers the filling so I don't include it. I often make a lot of these at one time and freeze the rest, defrosting them for a lovely breakfast or light lunch.

FILLING
1 ½ cups (375 mL) pitted, chopped Moroccan olives
1 ½ cups (375 mL) pitted, chopped royal olives
2 cups (500 mL) pitted, chopped kalamata olives
1 cup (250 mL) finely chopped onion
⅓ cup (80 mL) olive oil
1 ½ heaped Tbsp (22+ mL) dried mint

Ingredients continued…

In a small bowl, mix together the filling ingredients. Set aside.

In a large bowl, mix together the flour, mastic powder, mahleb powder and salt. Rub the vegetable shortening into the flour mixture with your fingers.

In another bowl, dilute the yeast with 1 cup (250 mL) milk and 1 Tbsp (15 mL) sugar. Cover this bowl with a kitchen towel and let rise for 15 minutes.

Mix together the remaining milk and sugar in a separate bowl. Lightly beat the egg and add to the bowl.

Add the yeast mixture to the flour mixture. Slowly mix the milk and egg mixture into the flour mixture with your hands until a dough is formed. Vigorously knead for 15 minutes until dough becomes smooth and elastic, then roll into a ball. Place the dough in a bowl, cover with plastic wrap and tea towels and let rise for 2 hours.

Recipe continued…

When the dough has risen, punch it down with your fists. Cut a piece the size of a tennis ball and roll it into a rectangle ⅛ inch (3 to 4 mm) thick and 8 ½ × 10 inches (22 × 25 cm) long. Place a heaped ½ cup (125+ mL) of the olive mixture in the lower half of the rectangle, leaving about ½ inch (1 cm) around the edges, then begin to roll up the dough.

On a flat surface, sprinkle a generous amount of sesame seeds and pour a little water overtop to wet them. Roll the finished loaf over the sesame seeds, covering it with seeds, including the bottom. Repeat with the remaining dough in the bowl. Once prepared, place the loaves, seam sides down, on a baking tray, cover with a kitchen towel and let rise for 1 hour.

Preheat oven to 325 °F (160 °C). Brush each loaf with egg wash just before baking and bake for 35 to 45 minutes.

Makes 4 to 5 loaves.

DOUGH

5 cups (1.25 L) all-purpose flour

½ tsp (2 mL) ground mastic powder

1 tsp (5 mL) ground mahleb powder

½ tsp (2 mL) salt

5 Tbsp (75 mL) vegetable shortening

1 envelope dry yeast (8 g)

1 ⅓ cups (310 mL) lukewarm milk, divided

1 ½ Tbsp (22 mL) sugar, divided

1 large egg

1 cup (250 mL) sesame seeds, for rolling in

1 egg, beaten for egg wash

CYPRIOT EASTER CHEESE BREAD (FLAOUNES)

Φλαούνες

Flaouna is a savoury Easter cheese bread unique to Cyprus. I still vividly remember my mom and her Cypriot best friend, Eleni, coming together every year in Canada to make what looked like enough flaounes to feed an entire Cypriot village. It is difficult to find the traditional cheese used to make flaounes outside of Cyprus, where it is simply known as "flaouna cheese" and is made from sheep and goat milk using a method similar to that used when making halloumi. In Canada, my mom and Eleni always had to improvise, and the result was a flaouna recipe that tasted even better than the traditional one. For this reason, I have included my mom's and Eleni's recipe here.

In Cyprus, sometimes raisins are omitted, or replaced with hemp seeds. Sometimes people make them in a square shape. I have found that people are quite passionate about their preferences. If you have any extra dough leftover, simply make little buns and bake them alongside the flaounes.

This is one of the most popular, if not the most popular recipe, on my blog. I always enjoy seeing the many photographs of readers' flaounes pop up in my social media accounts around Easter every year.

FILLING

In a large bowl, mix together the cheeses, mint, mastic powder, mahleb powder and baking powder. Add 3 eggs at a time and mix the cheese mixture together with your hands. Cover the bowl with a kitchen towel and let rest while you prepare the dough. Mix the sultanas into the filling mixture just before you are ready to roll out the dough for your first flaouna.

DOUGH

In a large bowl, mix together the flour, mastic powder, mahleb powder and salt. Rub the vegetable shortening into the flour mixture with your fingers.

In another bowl, dilute the yeast with 1 cup (250 mL) milk and 1 Tbsp (15 mL) sugar. Cover bowl with a kitchen towel and let rise for 15 minutes.

Recipe continued...

FILLING

3 cups (750 mL) grated kefalotyri cheese

2 ½ cups (625 mL) grated Parmigiano-Reggiano cheese

4 cups (1 L) grated Pecorino Romano cheese

2 Tbsp (30 mL) ground dry mint

1 ¼ tsp (6 mL) mastic powder

½ Tbsp (7 mL) mahleb powder

10 tsp (50 mL) baking powder

10 eggs

¾ cup (180 mL) sultanas

Ingredients continued...

Mix together the remaining milk and sugar and pour into a bowl. Lightly beat the egg, then add it to the milk mixture. Add the yeast mixture to the flour mixture. Slowly mix the milk mixture into the flour mixture with your hands until a dough is formed. Vigorously knead for 15 minutes until dough becomes smooth and elastic, then roll into a ball. Place the dough in a bowl, cover with plastic wrap and tea towels and let rise for 2 hours.

When the dough has risen, punch it down with your fists. Cut a piece of dough the size of a lemon (a little smaller than a tennis ball) and roll it out into a circle approximately 8 inches (20 cm) in diameter.

On a flat surface, sprinkle a generous amount of sesame seeds and pour a little water overtop to wet them. Press one side of the dough circle into the sesame seeds. Place 1 cup (250 mL) of the cheese mixture into the middle of the circle. Brush egg wash around the edge of the circular piece of dough. Fold the sides of the circle to form an open triangle. Lightly press the corner edges down with a fork to secure the cheese inside. Once prepared, place the breads on a baking tray, cover with a kitchen towel and let rise for 1 hour.

Heat oven to 325 °F (160 °C). Lightly brush the top of each pastry with egg wash and bake for 45 minutes.

Makes 10 to 12 flaounes.

DOUGH

5 cups (1.25 L) all-purpose flour

½ tsp (2 mL) ground mastic powder

1 tsp (5 mL) ground mahleb powder

½ tsp (2 mL) salt

5 Tbsp (75 mL) vegetable shortening

1 envelope dry yeast (8 g)

1 ⅓ cups (330 mL) lukewarm milk, divided

1 ½ Tbsp (22 mL) sugar, divided

1 large egg

1 cup (250 mL) sesame seeds, for rolling in

1 egg, beaten for egg wash

CYPRIOT CREPES (KATTIMERI)
Καττιμέρι

I think of kattimeri as a Cypriot version of a crepe with cinnamon and honey. It is an incredibly basic recipe, and a dish that was made and enjoyed by my aunts when they were young, partly because the ingredients were cheap. Nowadays, they are usually made by my aunt during times of celebration, such as large, joyous family gatherings, or the arrival of a relative from abroad. Kattimeri can be enjoyed as a snack, for breakfast or as a dessert. I usually drizzle extra honey on top of mine with cinnamon, and recommend doing so yourself!

6 cups (1.5 L) traditional Cypriot "village flour" (or bread flour) + extra for dusting
2 ½ cups (625 mL) lukewarm water
½ tsp (2 mL) salt
2 Tbsp (30 mL) + ½ tsp (2 mL) olive oil + extra for drizzling
1 tsp (5 mL) cinnamon
¾ cup (180 mL) sugar
sugar, for sprinkling between the crepes
honey, for serving

In a large bowl, mix together the flour, water, salt and olive oil until a dough is formed. Knead the dough vigorously for 10 minutes, then place in a lightly floured sealed plastic bag and let rest in a warm place for 45 minutes.

In a small bowl, mix together the cinnamon and sugar.

Once the dough is ready, take a lemon-sized amount (slightly larger than a golf ball, about 3 oz/95 g) and place on a liberally floured surface. Using a rolling pin, roll out the dough so that it becomes a very thin circle—about 1 mm thick and 14 inches (34 to 35 cm) in diameter. Ensure any excess flour is dusted off before proceeding.

In the centre of each circle, drizzle 4 tsp (20 mL) olive oil. Gently fold the circle in half so the top surace is coated in oil. Sprinkle 3 ½ tsp (17 mL) of the cinnamon mixture over the circle. Fold the circle into a square-sized envelope, about 6 ½ inches (17 cm) wide.

Recipe continued...

Heat a skillet on medium heat. Add 1 square at a time and let it cook for 1 minute before turning it over and cooking it on the other side for 1 minute, then turning it over again for 1 minute. The crepes are ready when they have brown spots on both sides. Stack the kattimeri one on top of the other, with a little sugar sprinkled between each crepe, until ready to serve. Serve with a drizzle of honey overtop.

Makes 14 to 16 crepes.

BUTTERNUT SQUASH PIES (KOLOKOTES)

Κολοκοτές

These delicious hand pies are typically made in the fall and winter when a particular variety of squash comes into season in Cyprus, and I look forward to making them every year. This squash grows over the summer, and the younger version of it is used when making fresh black-eyed peas (see p. 153), while in the fall it grows to be quite large and turns red. Squash will usually store throughout winter, and as such, these hand pies are made in both seasons in Cyprus. It is difficult to find this squash outside of Cyprus, so in Canada we use a combination of acorn and kabocha squash—varieties that won't become too mushy when cooked. This recipe doesn't contain any butter or eggs, and it is a recipe that my relatives will make if they are fasting for religious reasons and want to avoid dairy and egg products. Also note that the simple additions of sultana raisins and brown sugar do not transform these into a dessert. They remain very savoury in taste, with just a hint of sweetness, and they make a great breakfast, lunch or afternoon snack.

FILLING

Mix all filling ingredients together in a bowl and let rest for 2 hours.

DOUGH

In a large bowl, rub the flour and olive oil together with your fingers so that the flour absorbs the oil. Add the vinegar, salt and warm water, and mix the dough together with your hands. Add more flour and/or warm water if needed, so that you can form a ball. Shape the dough into a ball, place it in a lightly oiled bowl, cover the bowl with plastic wrap and 2 kitchen towels and let rest for 30 minutes.

Preheat oven to 375 °F (190 °C) and line 2 baking sheets with parchment paper.

Recipe continued...

FILLING

2 cups (500 mL) cubed acorn squash (½-inch/1-cm cubes)

2 cups (500 mL) cubed kabocha squash (½-inch/1-cm cubes)

1 shallot, lightly sautéed in 2 Tbsp (30 mL) olive oil

3 to 4 Tbsp (45 to 60 mL) chopped fennel fronds (the green leaves)

½ tsp (2 mL) pepper (or more to taste)

1 tsp (5 mL) salt

½ tsp (2 mL) cinnamon

1 Tbsp (15 mL) brown sugar

½ cup (125 mL) fine bulgur wheat

½ cup (125 mL) sultana raisins

Ingredients continued...

On a lightly floured surface, roll out the dough ¼ inch (5 mm) thick. Cut out circles with 6-inch (15 cm) diameters. Spoon ¼ cup (60 mL) filling into the lower half of each circle. Close the circles to form half-moon shapes, pressing the edges tightly together using your fingers. Let pies rest for about 15 minutes.

Brush the top of each pie with a little olive oil and cut out little holes. Bake for 30 to 40 minutes, until light golden brown on top.

Makes 12 small pies.

DOUGH

4 cups (1 L) all-purpose flour

¼ cup (60 mL) olive oil + extra for coating

1 Tbsp (15 mL) chardonnay vinegar (or any vinegar)

pinch of salt

1 ½ cups (375 mL) warm water

SPINACH PIES (SPANAKOPITES)

Σπανακόπιτες

You can find many different spinach pie recipes in Cyprus, but I prefer the individual-sized pies. When you strain the spinach mixture, don't throw away the strained juice—store it in the fridge or freezer and use it later in your vegetable soups; it adds a great flavour.

⅓ cup (80 mL) olive oil, for frying
1 heaped cup (250+ mL) finely chopped leeks
1 ½ cups (375 mL) finely chopped spring onions
¾ cup (180 mL) finely chopped dill
11 oz (310 g) baby spinach
1 tsp (5 mL) salt
¼ tsp (1 mL) pepper
1 large egg
1 ½ cups (375 mL) grated feta
16 phyllo sheets
(14 ½ × 18 inches/36 × 45 cm)
½ cup (125 mL) melted salted butter, for brushing

Heat the olive oil in a frying pan on the stove over medium-high heat. When hot, add the leeks, spring onions and dill and stirfry for 2 minutes. Add the spinach and continue to stirfry until spinach has wilted. Add salt and pepper. Strain the spinach mixture over a bowl for about 2 hours.

Preheat oven to 350 °F (175 °C) and line 2 baking pans with parchment paper.

In a large bowl, lightly beat the egg. Add the grated feta and cooled spinach mixture and stir together.

Place 1 sheet of phyllo on a flat surface. Brush the sheet with melted butter. Place another sheet of phyllo on top. Brush this sheet with melted butter. Slice the 2 phyllo sheets into 5 equal strips using a sharp knife. Place 1 tsp (5 mL) of the feta/spinach mixture onto each phyllo strip and fold them over again and again, creating small triangles. Use a little bit of butter to "glue" down any leftover phyllo hanging over the edge. Place each triangle onto the baking sheet and brush lightly with a little butter. Repeat with the remaining phyllo sheets until all 16 are used up. You may end up with a little extra phyllo or a little extra filling depending on how you have made them, and this is okay. It is not an exact science.

Place a baking sheet (one at a time) into the oven and bake for about 15 to 20 minutes until the edges of the triangles turn golden brown.

Makes 35 to 39 spinach triangles.

ZUCCHINI SPICE MUFFINS

I always end up with a lot of zucchini by the time September comes in Cyprus. This recipe may not be traditionally Cypriot, but it comes in very handy around that time, as I have found that a lot of people are looking for zucchini recipes to simply use up their excess zucchini. The same could be said for Canada, a phenomenon I experienced with the zucchini growing in my mom's garden. So, this simple zucchini muffin recipe comes in handy wherever you are!

Preheat oven to 350 °F (175 °C) and line a muffin tray with muffin cups.

In a large bowl, whisk together the eggs, oil, sugar and vanilla until well combined. Stir in the grated zucchini, then stir in the cinnamon, nutmeg, cardamom, baking powder, baking soda and salt. Fold in the flour to form a smooth batter. Stir in the orange zest, walnuts and chocolate chips. Divide the batter between 10 large muffin cups. Bake for 25 to 28 minutes.

Makes 10 large muffins.

2 small eggs

½ cup (125 mL) coconut oil

¾ cup (180 mL) brown sugar

1 tsp (5 mL) vanilla extract

1 cup (250 mL) finely grated zucchini, squeezed to drain the juice

1 ¼ tsp (6 mL) cinnamon

⅛ tsp (0.5 mL) ground nutmeg

⅛ tsp (0.5 mL) cardamom

½ tsp (2 mL) baking powder

½ tsp (2 mL) baking soda

½ tsp (2 mL) salt

1 ½ cups (375 mL) flour

1 tsp (5 mL) grated orange zest

⅓ cup (80 mL) roasted walnuts

⅓ cup (80 mL) chocolate chips

HALLOUMI MINT SCONES

In my imaginary bakery, these scones play a starring role. They are loved by everyone who tries them. This is perhaps one of my favourite modern Cypriot recipes—it uses the traditional Cypriot combination of mint and halloumi, which is found in a few of the traditional breads in Cyprus. This recipe, however, adopts a scone base, which I find easier and quicker to make. Same taste, just a bit faster. They make great breakfast scones and are best enjoyed when hot. If there are any leftover the next day, I usually heat them up in the oven, wrapped in tinfoil.

2 cups (500 mL) all-purpose flour
1 Tbsp (15 mL) baking powder
½ cup (125 mL) cold salted butter, chopped into small pieces
1 cup (250 mL) cubed halloumi pieces
¼ cup (60 mL) chopped fresh mint
1 large egg, lightly beaten
⅔ cup (160 mL) buttermilk

Preheat oven to 400 °F (200 °C) and line a baking sheet with parchment paper.

In a bowl, whisk together the flour and baking powder. Rub the butter into the flour mixture using your fingers to create a coarse meal. Add the halloumi and mint to the flour mixture and loosely mix together.

Mix the egg and buttermilk together and add to the flour mixture. Use your hands to create a soft, slightly sticky but still workable dough. Add a little more flour if necessary to get this texture. Do not overwork the dough.

Form 6 to 7 equally sized free-form scones and place them on the baking sheet. Flour your hands if the dough is sticky. Bake for 20 minutes until golden brown.

Makes 6 to 7 large scones.

HONEY CINNAMON STICKS (THAKTILA)

Δἀκτυλα

These are one of the first pastries I buy when I return to Cyprus after a long time away. The name literally translates to "ladies' fingers," and I honestly don't know how this name came about. When I hear "ladyfingers" in Canada, I typically think of the biscuits used to make tiramisu. These are different. These ladies' fingers are like little bite-sized, cylinder-like pastries. They have a sweet nutty filling and each bite fills your mouth with orange blossom, cinnamon and clove flavours. They are very close to being like a bite-sized baklava, but without the butter. They take a little bit of time to make, but are definitely worth it. They are absolutely delicious and I expect that you will not be able to eat just one!

DOUGH

In a large bowl, mix together the flours and salt. Add in the shortening and rub it between your fingers with the flour to combine. Make a little hole in the middle of your flour and add your egg. Slowly add the warm water. Knead the dough well for 10 minutes, until smooth and glossy. Shape the dough into a ball and place in a bowl, cover with plastic wrap and 2 tea towels and let rest for 1 hour.

FILLING

Mix the filling ingredients in a small bowl.

SYRUP

Slowly heat and stir the sugar, water, orange rind, cinnamon stick and cloves. Once the syrup reaches a low boil, simmer for 5 minutes, turn off the heat, add in the honey and stir. Let the syrup cool completely.

Recipe continued...

DOUGH

1 cup (250 mL) bread flour

1 cup (250 mL) all-purpose flour

pinch of salt

2 Tbsp (30 mL) vegetable shortening

1 egg, beaten

⅓ cup (80 mL) warm water (you may need more)

FILLING

1 ¼ cups (310 mL) coarsely chopped almonds

3 Tbsp (45 mL) sugar

¾ tsp (4 mL) cinnamon

Ingredients continued...

Roll the dough out, about ¼ inch (5 mm) thick. Place ½ tsp (2 mL) filling in a little rectangle piece of dough about 2 × 3 inches (5 × 8 cm). Fold the dough over lengthwise to cover the filling. Secure the edges using a fork. Repeat with the remaining dough.

On the stove, heat the vegetable oil for frying. Once hot, add the ladies' fingers a few at a time. Once they turn golden brown and have formed bubbles on top, remove with a slotted spoon and quickly dip into the cooled syrup. Remove from the syrup, let cool (about 5 to 10 minutes) on a piece of parchment paper, then enjoy. Ladies' fingers can be stored in a glass container once they have cooled.

Makes about 35 pastries.

SYRUP

2 cups (500 mL) sugar

1 cup (250 mL) water

1 orange rind peel (approx. ¾ inch or
    2 cm wide)

½ cinnamon stick

5 to 6 cloves

3 Tbsp (45 mL) honey

1 tsp (5 mL) lemon juice

2 tsp (10 mL) orange blossom water
    (optional)

vegetable oil, for frying

67

PORK PIES (BOUREKIA ME KIMA)
Πουρέκια με κιμά

My mom learned this recipe from my Godmother's family, who migrated to Cyprus from Antalya, Turkey. These boureki are in the traditional shape that my Godmother's family made them, although nowadays they are often sold as closed little semi-circular hand pies. Boureki make a wonderful savoury snack, but they are also great as an appetizer to a large meal.

DOUGH

1 cup (250 mL) all-purpose flour
1 cup (250 mL) traditional Cypriot "village flour" (or bread flour)
generous pinch of salt
1 Tbsp (15 mL) vegetable shortening
1 egg, lightly beaten
⅓ to ½ cup (80 to 125 mL) warm water

In a large bowl, stir together the flours and salt. Rub the vegetable shortening into the flour, pinching the ingredients together with your fingers. Make a well in the middle of the flour and add the beaten egg. Begin to mix together the egg and flour with a fork. Slowly add the warm water and mix the ingredients together until a dough forms. Vigorously knead the dough for 10 minutes then shape into a ball, place in a bowl, cover with plastic wrap and 2 tea towels and let rest for 1 hour.

FILLING

1 medium-sized onion, finely chopped
½ cup (125 mL) parsley, finely chopped
¾ lb (350 g) lean ground pork
1 ¼ tsp (6 mL) salt
½ tsp (2 mL) pepper

3 cups (750 mL) vegetable oil, for frying

In another bowl, add the onion, parsley, pork and salt and pepper. Mix well and keep the mixture refrigerated until the dough is ready.

Once the dough is ready, cut a small piece off and use a pasta machine or rolling pin to make a thin pastry dough (approx. 1 mm thin). Use a knife and cut out a small circle 4 inches (10 cm) in diameter. Place a teaspoon of the pork mixture in the middle of the circle and spread it thin with the back of your spoon. Leave a 1-inch (2.5 cm) space around the edge of the circle. Fold the edge of the circle over to create pleats around the pork mixture in the centre. Repeat until all dough is used up.

Once you have finished preparing all of the pies, heat your oil in a medium-sized frying pan. Once the oil is hot, add 7 to 10 pies at a time and deep fry for 2 minutes, until each side is golden brown. Drain on paper towels before serving, so that some of the oil can be absorbed.

Makes about 60 little pies.

TAHINI PIES (TAHINOPITES)
Ταχινόπιτες

Tahinopites are a traditional Cypriot bread made with tahini, cinnamon and sugar that I think would be extremely popular outside of Cyprus if more people knew about them. In the past, I remember being able to buy tahinopites off of the backs of bicycles when shopping in town, or even on the beach during the summer. Nowadays there are very few street vendors that continue to sell tahinopites this way, although all the bakeries around Cyprus continue to carry them. I struggled for many years to develop a recipe that yielded the gooey, flat, sweet tahinopites I remember from my childhood, so I am particularly proud of this recipe.

When I first started to make tahinopites, I often found they ended up too small, they rose too much and they were too dry. There are a few tricks I have learned over the years from seasoned tahinopita bakers, such as the importance of baking soda, letting the dough rest before you roll it out and the method by which you twist the rolls. Use brown (not black) tahini (tahini butter from unhulled seeds) if possible, but white tahini (tahini butter from hulled sesame seeds) works well too, so don't worry if you cannot find brown tahini. In Cyprus, it is usually possible to go to a bakery and ask to buy some brown tahini directly from the shop.

A special thank you to Agathi Ioannou, my aunt's friend who is a professional tahinopita baker, who took a full day a few years ago to teach me how to make these. This also happens to be one of my most popular blog recipes, and I am always so touched by how many people enjoy this recipe.

FILLING

1 cup (250 mL) brown tahini (or white tahini)
½ tsp (2 mL) vegetable oil
6 Tbsp (90 mL) white sugar
½ tsp (2 mL) cinnamon
⅛ tsp (0.5 mL) baking soda

Ingredients continued...

FILLING

Prepare your tahini filling. Add the ingredients together and stir. The texture should be a bit rough.

DOUGH

In a large bowl, combine the flours, salt, baking soda and vegetable oil. Use a tablespoon of warm water to dilute the dry yeast, then add this to the mixing bowl. Using a dough hook on your mixer, mix the ingredients together (about 1 to 2 minutes). Continue to mix for about 5 to 8 minutes and slowly add the water. Do not overknead. The dough should come together as a smooth ball, with a slight shine to it.

Recipe continued...

70

DOUGH

1 cup (250 mL) + 1 scant cup
(under 250 mL) traditional Cypriot
"village flour" (or bread flour)

¼ cup (60 mL) "00" flour
(or all-purpose flour)

½ tsp (2 mL) salt

¼ tsp (1 mL) baking soda

2 Tbsp (30 mL) vegetable oil

¾ to 1 cup (180 to 250 mL) warm water

½ tsp (2 mL) active dry yeast

You may need to adjust the water (a little less or a little more) depending on when your dough forms a ball. Place the dough into a lightly oiled bowl, cover with plastic wrap and let rest for 20 minutes.

Once the dough is ready, divide into 6 equal pieces. Using a rolling pin, roll out 1 piece of dough into a rectangle about 8 × 10 inches (20 × 25 cm). Spoon about 3 Tbsp (45 mL) of the tahini mixture into the middle of the rectangle and spread it out thinly, covering all of the dough except for ½ inch (1 cm) around the edge. Fold the bottom of the rectangle to the top, leaving a ½-inch (1 cm) lip at the top to fold down and creating an envelope-like shape. From the bottom of the rectangle, roll the rectangle up to create a long cylinder shape, which you will then stretch out with your hands to about 16 inches (40 cm). Twist the cylinder so it starts to swirl, then fold the swirled cylinder in half and roll it out again while continuing to twist each end in opposite directions to create more of a swirl stick pattern. Continue rolling until the length of the cylinder is about 8 inches (20 cm, less is okay too). Some of the tahini mixture may squeeze out during the rolling, but this is okay—it is supposed to be a bit messy. Curl the ends of the cylinder in opposite directions (creating an "S" shape) and take one end and place it on top of the other.

Make the other tahini pies the same way. Using a rolling pin, flatten each tahini pie into a flat disc about 8 inches (20 cm) or less across, then place on a baking tray lined with parchment paper. Let rise for 15 minutes and heat oven to 325 °F (160 °F). Place pies in the oven for about 20 minutes. Pies are ready when they are lightly brown on top and sound hollow if you tap the bottom.

Makes 6 tahini pies.

CAROB HONEY BRAN MUFFINS

I am a big fan of a really good bran muffin. I don't enjoy them overly sweet, and I like them to rise as much as possible instead of being flat and dense. When I was living in Cyprus, I couldn't find bran muffins anywhere, so I began making them myself using Cypriot yogurt and honey with carob flavouring in it. The carob honey flavour adds that bit of molasses-like texture to the muffin.

Carob flavour is distinct. It is more similar to butterscotch and caramel than to molasses or chocolate (which it is often suggested as a substitute for). But don't worry, you can still make these bran muffins with regular honey if carob honey isn't available. This recipe also calls for coconut oil, which will shine through in the end. Alternately, you can just use vegetable oil (substitute for the coconut oil) if you wish, which will yield more of a traditional bran muffin flavour. Overall, these muffins are large, moist, flavourful and delicious.

Preheat oven to 350 °F (175 °C).

In a small bowl, mix together the yogurt and baking soda. Let rest while you prepare the other ingredients. The yogurt mixture will rise a bit.

In a large bowl, mix together the flour, bran, ground pecans, baking powder, vanilla powder and salt.

In another large bowl, beat together the eggs, brown sugar, coconut oil, vegetable oil and honey for 5 minutes. Alternate adding the dry flour mixture and the yogurt mixture to the egg mixture, starting and ending with the dry mixture. Fold in the sultana raisins.

Scoop the mixture into each muffin cup about three-quarters of the way up. Bake for about 30 to 35 minutes, until a toothpick inserted in the centre of a muffin comes out clean. Let the tray cool for 2 minutes, then remove each muffin and place on a wire rack to cool completely.

Makes 18 large muffins.

2 cups (500 mL) strained Cypriot or Greek yogurt

2 tsp (10 mL) baking soda

2 cups (500 mL) all-purpose flour

2 cups (500 mL) wheat bran

2 Tbsp (30 mL) finely ground pecans

4 tsp (20 mL) baking powder

½ tsp (2 mL) vanilla powder

½ tsp (2 mL) salt

2 eggs

1 cup (250 mL) dark brown sugar

½ cup (125 mL) coconut oil

½ cup (125 mL) vegetable oil

¼ cup (60 mL) carob honey

¼ cup (60 mL) sultana raisins

BULGUR WHEAT PORK ROLLS (KOUPES)

Κούπες

A koupa is like a meaty, savoury doughnut made with bulgur wheat, spices and ground meat. A vegetarian version can also be made or purchased using mushrooms instead of ground meat, but I have included the meat version below as it is my favourite and one that my family sometimes still makes. Most often, koupes are eaten for breakfast with a squeeze of lemon overtop—in fact, you will find lemon wedges in bakeries alongside the pies for this purpose. In Cyprus, people rarely make these pies themselves anymore, as they take time and it can be a bit tricky ensuring that the koupa keeps its shape. Nowadays, every bakery will sell these, and there are some well-known places that specialize in making them. No visit or stay in Cyprus is complete without having enjoyed a breakfast of a koupa or two. Please note that if you can't find extra fine bulgur wheat, you can simply put the bulgur wheat in a food processor and process it until it is extra fine in texture, similar to sand granules.

SHELL

In a large bowl, add the bulgur wheat, salt and boiling water. Cover the bowl with plastic wrap and let rest for 1 ½ to 2 hours, until the bulgur wheat absorbs the water. Once the wheat mixture is ready, mix in the cinnamon, flour and white pepper.

FILLING

While the bulgur is resting, toast the pine nuts in a small pan on the stove. Once toasted, leave the pine nuts to the side to cool.

Heat 3 Tbsp (45 mL) olive oil in a pan, add the onion and cook and stir until soft. Add the pork and stirfry until cooked and any liquid has evaporated. Add the toasted pine nuts, parsley, mint, cumin, cinnamon, allspice and salt and pepper to taste.

Begin to prepare the koupes. Add a drop of water to your hands and rub them together. Take a walnut-sized amount of the bulgur wheat mixture and spread it out into your hands. You may need to add more

Recipe continued...

SHELL

2 cups (500 mL) extra fine bulgur wheat

1 tsp (5 mL) salt

3 ½ cups (875 mL) boiling water

½ tsp (2 mL) cinnamon

½ cup (125 mL) all-purpose flour

½ tsp (2 mL) white pepper

Ingredients continued...

water if the mixture cracks too much. Flatten the bulgur wheat mixture with the palms of your hands, then curl your hand to form a little bowl shape and add a teaspoon of filling into the bowl. Add a little bit more bulgur wheat mixture on top of the meat. With both hands, form a small, tightly packed little oval ball. Make sure the sphere is tightly packed, otherwise the koupa might fall apart when you fry it. Place the koupa on a plate and prepare additional koupes the same way.

In a frying pan, add vegetable oil until about 2 ¾ inches (7 cm) deep. Add one koupa at a time, rolling occasionally in the vegetable oil to make sure it becomes golden brown all the way around. Once the koupa is golden brown, remove it and place it on a paper towel to soak up the excess vegetable oil.

Makes 20 to 25 koupes.

FILLING*

2 Tbsp (30 mL) toasted pine nuts

olive oil, for frying, divided

1 finely chopped large onion

1 lb (500 g) lean ground pork

½ cup (125 mL) finely chopped parsley

2 Tbsp (30 mL) finely chopped
   fresh mint

½ tsp (2 mL) cumin

¾ tsp (4 mL) cinnamon

⅛ tsp (0.5 mL) allspice

salt and pepper, to taste

Note: This recipe yields 1 ½ cups (375 mL) extra filling, which can be enjoyed as a main served over boiled bulgur wheat with some tashi (p. 180) or multiply the shell ingredients by one and a half in order to use up all the filling.

TRADITIONAL SESAME BREAD RINGS (KOULOURIA)

Κουλούρια

My mom told me that back in the "old days," vendors would sell a bunch of these strung together on a string, handing them out from a cart, and my grandfather would buy them for her as a special treat when she was a child. Koulouria are a savoury bread, hard and crunchy on the outside and soft on the inside. They have a spicy, nutty flavour to them because of the spices used: sesame, anise and nigella seeds. They make a delicious meal on their own when paired with a simple olive oil or a dip of some sort (like tashi, p. 180), and are a popular favourite breakfast snack to this day in Cyprus (you can find them in any bakery). Though they may look difficult to make, they are quite easy. I use a mixer to knead the dough, which makes this recipe significantly easier, but if you prefer making them by hand you can do so, it will just take longer.

BREAD

4 cups (1 L) bread flour

½ Tbsp (7 mL) salt

¼ tsp (1 mL) ground cumin seeds

¼ + ⅛ tsp (1.5 mL) ground anise seeds

1 Tbsp (15 mL) sugar

1 ¼ cups + 3 Tbsp (355 mL) warm water

2 Tbsp (30 mL) olive oil

1 envelope instant quick rise yeast (8 g)

TOPPING

½ tsp (2 mL) cumin seeds

½ tsp (2 mL) anise seeds

½ cup (125 mL) sesame seeds

2 tsp (10 mL) nigella seeds

1 Tbsp (15 mL) water

BREAD

In the bowl of a mixer, stir together the bread flour, salt, cumin, anise and sugar.

In a small bowl, mix together the water and olive oil, then add into the mixer. Add in the yeast. Knead the dough using the dough hook on your mixer, or by hand, until the dough becomes smooth and shiny. This will take about 10 to 15 minutes if using a mixer. Place the dough back into a bowl, cover it with plastic wrap and let it rest for 15 minutes in a warm place. It will rise.

TOPPING

In a separate large flat dish, add the topping ingredients and mix together with a fork, ensuring the water touches all the seeds. Line a baking sheet with parchment paper and preheat oven to 375 °F (190 °C).

Recipe continued...

Divide the dough into 8 to 10 pieces and roll them into long cylinders about 18 inches (45 cm) long. Roll each cylinder over the topping seeds to cover them all over, then shape into rings and pinch the ends together to close the ring. Place rings on the baking sheet and cover with a kitchen towel. Leave the rolls to rise with the kitchen towel over them for 1 hour. You can brush with milk before you place them in the oven, but it is not necessary.

Bake for about 20 minutes, until golden brown on top. The rolls are ready if they sound hollow when you tap the bottom once they come out.

Makes 8 to 10 pastries.

Soups, Salads & Small Bites

This would not be a Cypriot cookbook if I didn't include some of the many small dishes, salads and side foods that are enjoyed there.

Traditional Cypriot salads are simple but ever-changing. My family would probably insist that they do not have any salad "recipes" per se, as salad is whatever greens and vegetables are in season dressed simply with homemade olive oil or red wine vinegar or lemon juice (this is how I dress the majority of my salads to this day). As a result, a Cypriot salad changes depending on the time of year—in the summer you might find a large bowl of purslane with cucumber and mint; in the winter it might be a large bowl filled with baby Cyprus vetch or a local variety of cabbage with lemon juice.

Soups are most often enjoyed during a very short time period over winter and early spring, and are stand-alone meals in and of themselves. As for the various sides and small snacks, there are too many to list here. Below, however, you will find my favourites.

TOMATO AND FETA SALAD

This salad is something you might find as an appetizer in a taverna, but that's not how I first discovered it—I first made this salad after purchasing an excess of beautiful organic pomodoro tomatoes from an organic market in Limassol. I had some friends over for a roast chicken dinner one night, and one of my friends saw the beautifully sweet tomatoes. They put together a quick salad that could feed many people and would pair well with a nice meat dish. The key to making this simple salad taste great is the combination of sweet tomatoes with the tang of wild oregano and excellent-quality balsamic vinegar. It's a very simple salad, but one that is useful to have. The recipe is best enjoyed when tomatoes are in season. If you wish, you can garnish the salad with pickled caper shoots (kapari) too.

Slice the tomatoes into ¼-inch (5 mm) thick slices. Sprinkle the crumbled feta and diced red onion on top of the tomatoes. Drizzle the ingredients with olive oil and balsamic vinegar. Season with salt and pepper to taste. Garnish with dried oregano and serve.

Makes 2 to 3 servings.

About 6 to 8 sweet pomodoro tomatoes (or other sweet, meaty tomatoes)
1 ¾ cups (430 mL) crumbled feta
½ red onion, finely diced
1 to 2 Tbsp (15 to 30 mL) excellent-quality olive oil
1 to 2 Tbsp (15 to 30 mL) excellent-quality balsamic vinegar
salt and pepper, to taste
dried wild oregano, as garnish

PURSLANE SALAD (SALATA GLYSTIRIDA)
Σαλάτα γλιστρίδα

This is one of my favourite Cypriot summer salads—it's simple and refreshing and incredibly easy to make. Although purslane can be found in North America, I often only see it being used in soups. I include it here because I think that a fresh recipe might be enjoyed by many. Purslane is best enjoyed as fresh as possible, otherwise the leaves will begin to wilt. You can also add tomato and lettuce to the salad and it will taste just as good. There are at least two different varieties of purslane that I know of, but don't worry too much about this as this salad will work with any type of edible purslane.

In a large bowl, add the purslane and cucumber. Add the dried mint, red wine vinegar, olive oil and salt and toss together.

Makes 2 servings.

2 cups (500 mL) purslane leaves
  (1 small bunch)
1 Persian cucumber, diced (approx.
  1 cup/250 mL, measured once diced)
¾ tsp (4 mL) dried mint
1 Tbsp (15 mL) red wine vinegar
1 ½ Tbsp (22 mL) olive oil
salt, to taste

CYPRIOT POTATO SALAD (PATATOSALADA)
Πατατοσαλάτα

I am told by my mom that when my grandparents left to tend the animals in the fields, they would often take the ingredients for potato salad and make this on the side as they watched over the animals. It was considered a "poor man's" lunch, but the fact is that this salad is really delicious and healthy, and is one that we often make at home when craving something hearty, healthy and fast.

Cyprus is known for its potatoes because of the red soil in which they are grown. It is the soil that gives the Cyprus potato a unique rich, earthy and buttery taste. There are different varieties of Cypriot potatoes, but when I have seen them sold outside of Cyprus, particularly in the UK, they are often referred to as "Cypriot potatoes" and you can identify them by their dark brown spots and slightly reddish appearance. However, if you can't find Cypriot potatoes that's not a problem, and I have used fingerling potatoes as a substitute in the recipe. Another trick if you have the time is to smash the potatoes apart using a fork rather than dicing them. This will leave ridges in the potatoes, which help to soak up the dressing and make each bite more flavourful.

1 lb (450 g) fingerling potatoes (or another variety of small- to medium-sized potatoes)
1 cup (250 mL) diced celery (approx. 2 inches/5 cm thick)
¼ cup (60 mL) diced celery leaves
¼ cup (60 mL) diced spring onions
½ cup (125 mL) diced tomato
⅓ cup (80 mL) diced cucumber
4 hard boiled eggs, cooled and diced
⅓ cup (80 mL) olive oil
1 ¼ tsp (6 mL) salt
1 scant Tbsp (under 15 mL) dried mint
2 ½ Tbsp (37 mL) red wine vinegar

Boil the potatoes until cooked and let cool. Dice into large bite-sized pieces. Add potatoes to a large bowl and combine with all of the remaining salad ingredients. Toss together and enjoy.

Makes 3 to 4 side servings.

WATERMELON AND HALLOUMI

(KARPOUZI ME HALLOUMI)

Καρπούζι με χαλλούμι

It is quite common to find a serving of watermelon and halloumi on my family's table at breakfast or in the afternoon in the summer—not as a salad per se, but just as an option to eat at any time. This is not so much a recipe as it is a delicious "sweet and salty" snack found everywhere in Cyprus and, despite its simplicity, I think it deserves to be included in a Cypriot Cookbook because of its popularity. Also, I have seen a lot of people abroad enjoy the combination of salty feta and watermelon, but I have always wondered why the same delicious combination of salty halloumi and sweet watermelon has not been discovered! So, I thought it would be nice to share the idea.

Simply serve the two together and enjoy.

Makes as much as you like.

watermelon slices (use as many as you wish)
halloumi slices (use as many as you wish)

CACTUS PEAR FRUIT SALAD

In Amargeti, I watch every summer as the colours of the cactus pears change from green to red to yellow. In Cyprus, cactus pears are usually enjoyed just as they are, chilled for breakfast on a hot summer's morning. With that said, I didn't feel that I could really include chilled cactus fruit as a recipe! I occasionally enjoy jazzing cactus fruit up a bit with orange juice and lime rinds, and for me this salad is a welcome treat, if only because I have to wait patiently every year to make it (and because I appreciate how difficult it is to gather). I remember my aunts going out with a special contraption consisting of a long stick with an open can at the end to carefully pick this fruit (and then, even more carefully, to clean it). Like many Cypriot kids, I learned the hard way what happens if you grab a cactus pear straight from the tree—don't do it! In Cyprus, we have the yellow variety of cactus pears, but it is okay to use the red variety as well. This salad dressing works with other fruit salads of your choice, too.

¼ cup (60 mL) freshly squeezed orange juice
½ tsp (2 mL) lime juice
1 tsp (5 mL) sugar
pinch of vanilla powder
1 Tbsp (15 mL) fresh mint, finely chopped
4 cactus pears, chilled, peeled and quartered
grated lime, as garnish

In a small bowl, add the orange juice, lime juice, sugar, vanilla powder and mint. Stir the dressing until the sugar has dissolved. Place the cleaned, chilled cactus pear in a bowl, pour the salad dressing overtop, garnish with grated lime and enjoy.

Makes 2 to 3 servings.

TOMATO SOUP WITH ORZO

I love the tomatoes that grow in Cyprus, so I often find myself making tomato soup when the weather begins to cool down. This is not a traditional Cypriot recipe, but one that I enjoy simply because it makes use of the delicious fresh produce found there, and it is a reliable tomato soup recipe. I have also added orzo pasta to this recipe—we use a lot of orzo pasta in Cyprus, and this adds an extra layer of comfort for me. Sometimes I will serve this soup alongside a grilled halloumi sandwich (my Cypriot version of the classic combination of tomato soup and grilled cheese!).

1 Tbsp (15 mL) olive oil
2 Tbsp (30 mL) salted butter
2 shallots, finely chopped
1 large garlic clove, finely chopped
1 tsp (5 mL) all-purpose flour
1 tsp (5 mL) tomato paste
two 14-oz (400 mL) cans chopped tomatoes
2 large tomatoes, chopped
1 bay leaf
3 cups (750 mL) chicken broth
1 tsp (5 mL) brown sugar
⅓ cup (80 mL) chopped fresh basil + extra for garnish
salt and pepper, to taste
8 tsp (40 mL) whipping cream or Greek yogurt (optional) + extra for garnish
¼ cup (60 mL) orzo pasta

In a large pot, heat the olive oil and butter over medium heat. Add the shallots and garlic and fry until translucent. Add the flour and fry for 1 minute, until the flour is cooked. Add the tomato paste, chopped tomatoes, fresh tomatoes, bay leaf and broth. Stir in the sugar and fresh basil. Season with salt and pepper to taste. Simmer on low for 30 minutes.

Boil your orzo pasta in a separate pot filled with salted water until al dente. Remove the bay leaf from the tomato soup. Transfer the soup mixture to a blender and pulse until blended, then return soup to the pot. If you wish, stir in whipping cream or Greek yogurt to make it creamier. Stir in the drained orzo pasta. Garnish with a tablespoon of cream or yogurt and finely chopped basil.

Makes 4 servings.

SOURED WHEAT SOUP WITH HALLOUMI (TRAHANA)

Τραχανάς

Most people have a love or hate relationship with this soup. It has a soured smell and doesn't look entirely pleasant. I'll be honest, when I was a child, my mother couldn't make me swallow even one spoonful. But now, as an adult, I find myself making this all the time, especially once the weather turns. If you are on the love side of this, it is a lovely, comforting soup that is similar to a porridge and particularly soothing in the winter. The soup is called trahana and is made by boiling dried pieces of cracked wheat that have been mixed together with soured unpasteurized goat and/or sheep milk, salt and in some cases strained Greek yogurt, then leaving these pieces to dry in the sun. These dried pieces of cracked wheat and soured milk/yogurt (also referred to as "trahana") are then boiled in chicken stock to make trahana soup.

Traditionally, the pieces of cracked wheat were made in the late summer months. This is because milk sours easily in the heat, which averages about 35 to 40 °C outside, and about 25 °C inside a typical traditional Cypriot kitchen. The flavour of trahana will depend on various factors: the type of milk used, how long the milk is left to sour and whether salt is added when making the pieces of cracked wheat and soured milk/yogurt.

I have not included the process for making the actual pieces of cracked wheat and soured milk/yogurt here, as it is long and complicated, although I have included some pictures of my aunt making it for those interested. What I have done is include the recipe of how to boil the pieces of cracked wheat and soured milk/yogurt to get a nice creamy soup, as I still get asked questions on how to make the actual soup. There are slight variations on how this particular soup is enjoyed in Cyprus. In our family, we enjoy it simply with cubed halloumi and occasionally a little grated tomato.

Soak trahana pieces in the water overnight in a pot. The next day, add the chicken stock cube to the pot and simmer for about 40 minutes, until it turns into a creamy soup. (You can also omit the soaking stage and use homemade chicken stock or water with a chicken stock cube, boiling the pieces of trahana until it turns into a creamy soup. If opting to do this, it will just take longer for the soup to cook.)

Just before serving, add chopped halloumi. You may also wish to add 1 grated tomato to the soup. If so, add the tomato about 30 minutes into cooking, whether you let the pieces of trahana soak or not.

Makes 1 serving.

1 ½ oz (40 g) trahana pieces

2 ½ cups (625 mL) water or homemade chicken stock

1 chicken stock cube (omit if using homemade chicken stock)

2 Tbsp (30 mL) chopped halloumi

1 grated tomato (optional)

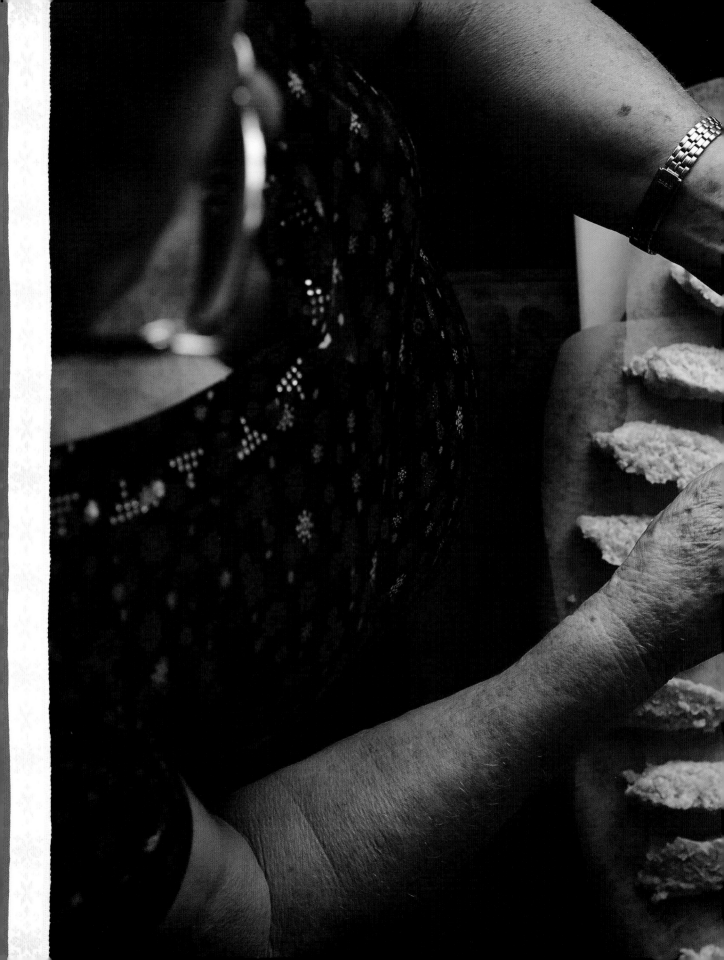

AVGOLEMONO SOUP

(SOUPA AVGOLEMONO)

Σούπα αυγολέμονο

There are countless recipes for avgolemono soup available out there, to the point where I questioned whether to include this recipe. However, the truth is that this is an important recipe in Cypriot cuisine in our family. Not only does it make for a soothing winter soup or comfort a cold, it is also traditionally served after Midnight Mass during Easter. To this day, my family attends Midnight Mass at the church in my mother's village, and using only candlelight, wanders back up to the house to all sit in the kitchen after midnight and enjoy large bowls of avgolemono. This is one Cypriot recipe that I have modified slightly: I have added peas and parsley to make the soup even heartier, which is how my mom and I make it in Canada. If you wish to make the traditional version, simply omit the peas and parsley.

2 carrots

1 celery stick

½ whole chicken (or 2 large chicken thighs and 3 drumsticks)

1 Tbsp (15 mL) salt, or to taste

½ Tbsp (7 mL) peppercorns

1 bay leaf

½ onion

8 cups (2 L) water

⅔ cup (160 mL) long grain rice

2 eggs

juice of 1 ½ lemons

½ cup + 1 Tbsp (140 mL) cold water, divided

1 cup (250 mL) peas, for garnish

5 stalks parsley, diced, for garnish

pepper, to taste

Add carrots, celery, chicken, salt, peppercorns, bay leaf and onion to a pot with 8 cups (2 L) water. Boil until chicken is cooked, skimming off any foam produced. Strain stock. Peel the meat off the chicken and set aside.

Place stock back in the pot on the stove. Add rice and boil until just cooked. Whisk eggs, lemon juice and 1 Tbsp (15 mL) cold water in a medium bowl. Add ½ cup (125 mL) cold water to the rice and stock mixture, then remove from heat.

Ladle a little stock into the egg/lemon mixture, whisking it constantly to prevent the egg from curdling. Once tempered (about 10 ladles), pour the mixture back into the pot, still whisking constantly for about 2 minutes. When serving, add chicken pieces, peas, diced parsley and lots of cracked pepper to each bowl as garnish.

Makes 4 to 5 servings.

TOMATO BULGUR WHEAT PILAF (POURGOURI)

Πουργούρι

This is a very popular side dish often served with Cypriot yogurt and alongside keftedes (see p. 156). Some people make it with canned tomatoes, but I prefer ripe, fresh tomatoes. In Cyprus, a lot of people will add one chicken bouillon cube to the pourgouri; you can go ahead and add half a chicken bouillon cube instead of salt if you wish, but personally I prefer to just add salt. Although traditionally a side dish, I think this dish is good enough to be enjoyed as a main course. To do so, I pair it with a side of feta cheese, anchovies and olives.

Heat the olive oil in a medium-sized pot over medium-high heat on the stove. Once hot, add the onion and shallots and fry for 2 minutes. Add the vermicelli and fry for about 3 minutes, until the vermicelli turns opaque and is slightly browned. Do not let the shallots or vermicelli burn.

Add the bulgur wheat and stir until coated in the oil. Add the blended tomatoes, 1 ½ cups (375 mL) water and salt. Simmer with a lid on the pot, occasionally stirring so the mixture doesn't stick. Check on the mixture and add more water if the mixture is sticking to the bottom of the pot.

Cook for 15 to 20 minutes, until the bulgur wheat is almost cooked, then remove pot from the heat, stir the pilaf, place the lid back on with a paper towel between the lid and the pot and let the pot sit for another 10 minutes before serving.

Makes 4 servings.

3 Tbsp (45 mL) olive oil

⅓ cup (80 mL) finely diced onion

¼ cup (60 mL) finely diced shallots (approx. 1 shallot)

¼ cup (60 mL) vermicelli, cut into pieces about ½ inch (1 to 1.5 cm) long

1 cup (250 mL) fine bulgur wheat

2 ⅓ cups (580 mL) blended tomatoes

1 ½ to 2 cups (375 to 500 mL) water

salt, to taste

HALLOUMI
AND ANARI (HALLOUMI KAI ANARI)
Χαλλούμι και αναρή

Halloumi is such an integral part of Cypriot cuisine. In recent years it has become increasingly popular outside Cyprus, too. My grandma used to pride herself on her halloumi, selling it as a means to make money. I remember going to the village and watching her sit on her chair with a large pot in front of her, making halloumi every day.

This is a valuable recipe to me, both on a personal level and also because it is very uncommon in Cyprus for halloumi makers to actually divulge their recipe, as most who still know how to make it, make it to sell. If you don't already know, freshly made halloumi is very soft and not as rubbery as store-bought, and I am sure if people outside Cyprus knew what it tasted like fresh it would be even more popular than it already is! I have included this recipe only for preservation purposes for those with an interest in how my family makes halloumi. Do not treat this as a recipe to try yourself. If you wish to learn how to make halloumi and Anari for yourself I would recommend taking a course in Cyprus or finding someone who knows how to make it, as it can be a bit tricky.

Place 23 cups (5.75 L) milk in a large pot on the stove. Take a little milk out of the pot and dilute the rennet and salt in the milk. Heat the milk so it becomes lukewarm, take it off the heat, add the rennet mixture and stir to incorporate. Cover the pot with a cloth and let it stand for about 30 minutes.

With clean hands, gently press the curds that have begun to form on the top of the mixture down to the bottom of the pot. Using both your hands, take out 2 cups (500 mL) of curd and place in a cheese strainer on a pan. Very gently press down on the curds to squeeze out some of the liquid (whey). Repeat until you have enough curds for about 5 strainers. Pour any whey drained into the bottom of the pan back into the pot. About 7 minutes after letting the curds rest in the cheese strainers, gently turn them over in their strainers. Strain for a further 5 minutes, then pour 1 cup (250 mL) cold water over the curds. Let rest for another 10 minutes. Remove the curds (halloumi) from the strainers and place them onto an empty sheet pan to rest. Pour any excess liquid from the bottom of the pan back into the pot.

24 cups (6 L) unpasteurized sheep
   and/or goat milk, divided
¼ tsp (1 mL) powdered rennet
½ tsp (2 mL) salt
1 cup (250 mL) water
½ cup (125 mL) sea salt

Recipe continued...

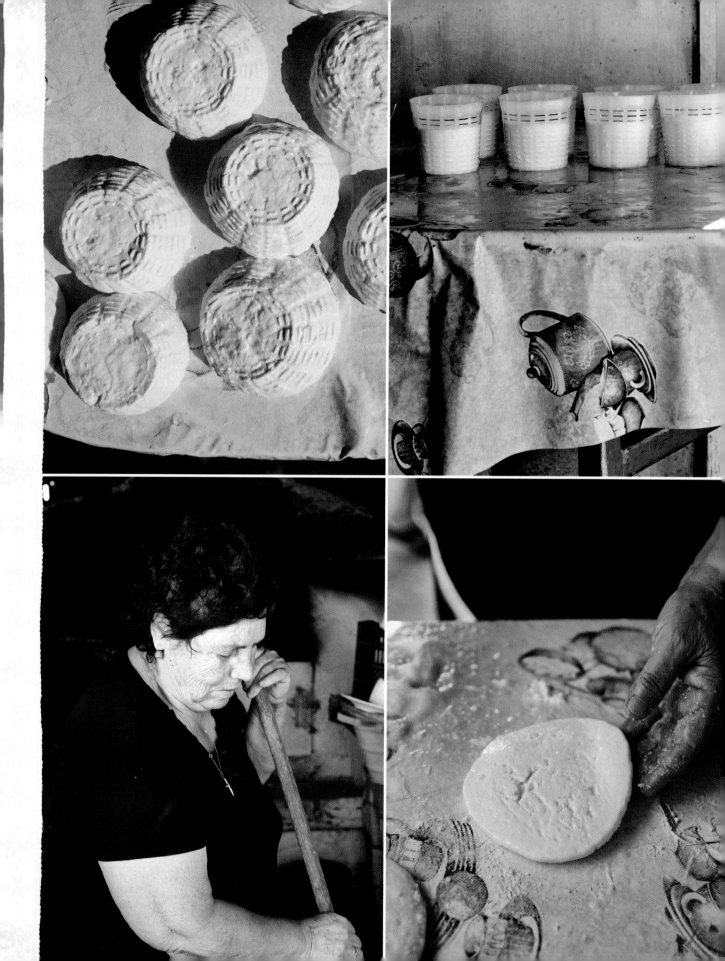

While the halloumi is resting, make the Anari. Place the pot with the liquid onto a hot stove. Once the liquid is hot, add the remaining 1 cup (250 mL) milk. Gently stir the mixture with a large wooden spoon. After 15 minutes, Anari will begin to float at the top of the liquid. Turn the heat down to low, place the wooden spoon in the middle of the pot and wobble it for 5 minutes. Using a slotted spoon, remove the Anari and place it in a cheese strainer so that it can drain into a pan.

Turn the heat under the pot up again and add the halloumi. Gently stir the pot and continue to cook for 20 minutes. Once the halloumi floats to the top, stop stirring and let it cook for another 10 minutes. The halloumi is ready when each piece looks like a sponge—the surface should spring back when you touch it.

Remove halloumi from the pot, place it in a pan and rub a very generous pinch of sea salt on each side of the cheese. Fold the halloumi pieces in half and place in a sterilized air-tight container filled with liquid from the pot. Store in the fridge.

Makes 5 halloumi and 1 Anari.

ZUCCHINI, EGGS AND POTATOES (PATATES ME AVGA)

Πατάτες με αυγά

One of my favourite Cypriot comfort foods is literally fried eggs and potatoes. There is another Cypriot side dish that consists of fried eggs and zucchini, and I occasionally fuse the two recipes together, making a heartier meal out of the two separate dishes. Make sure you fry the zucchini in a separate pan, as this ensures it does not end up soggy.

vegetable oil, for frying (enough for a ½ inch/1 cm depth)
2 medium potatoes, peeled and cut into 2 ½- × ½-inch (6 × 1 cm) strips (should be ¾ lb/350 g when cut)
3 Tbsp (45 mL) olive oil, for frying
1 ½ cups (375 mL) finely diced marrow zucchini, deseeded (5 oz/150 g once diced)
1 tsp (5 mL) fresh rosemary, finely chopped
4 eggs, lightly beaten
generous amounts salt and pepper, to taste

Pour ½ inch (1 cm) vegetable oil into a medium-sized pot over medium-high heat on the stove. Once hot, fry the potatoes until golden brown and cooked through. Remove the potatoes with a slotted spoon and place on paper towels to soak up some of the oil.

In a different small frying pan over high heat, add the olive oil and fry the zucchini until light brown. Add the potatoes and rosemary to the pan. Add the eggs and salt and pepper, stirring the mixture with a wooden spoon in order to break up the eggs. Serve immediately.

Makes 2 servings.

SHELLED WHITE BEAN SOUP (FASOLIA YACHNI)

Φασόλια γιαχνί

There are a large variety of vegetable dishes made in Cyprus, many of which incorporate tomato sauce. My aunt makes a version of this soup that I love, and I enjoy it with big pieces of bread to soak up the sauce at the end. This recipe is loosely based off of my aunt's recipe, but the flavours are more intense. There are more ingredients for more flavour in this recipe, and it is more soup than stew. In Cyprus, we use beans called xegounia, which are fresh white beans that have not yet dried out. However, I prefer this soup with frozen fresh borlotti beans, which is what I have used below, although you can use any type of frozen, fresh or dried small white beans (dried white beans will take longer to cook, so you may wish to soak them overnight). Don't forget to enjoy this soup with a big slice of bread to soak up the sauce at the end.

Place the beans in 4 cups (1 L) water and bring to a boil. Once the water has boiled, drain the water out, add 6 cups (1.5 L) water and boil the beans until half-cooked, about 30 minutes.

Add the rest of the ingredients all at the same time and simmer the soup for 35 to 40 minutes, until the vegetables are cooked. Note that if you are using dried beans, it may take longer to cook the beans and you may have to add more water when you add the vegetables.

Makes 5 servings.

2 ½ cups (625 mL) frozen fresh borlotti beans (approx. 14 oz/400 g) or any type of dried small white bean

10 cups (2.5 L) water, divided

1 cup (250 mL) finely chopped onion

1 cup (250 mL) finely chopped carrots (into little cubes)

1 cup (250 mL) finely chopped celery (into little cubes)

½ cup (125 mL) finely chopped fresh fennel

⅓ cup (80 mL) finely chopped fresh dill

¼ cup (60 mL) fennel leaves, finely chopped

¾ cup (180 mL) finely diced red pepper

3 cups (750 mL) fresh tomato purée

2 garlic cloves, finely chopped

¼ tsp (1 mL) sugar

pinch of hot pepper flakes

1 medium potato, chopped into cubes

¼ tsp (1 mL) freshly ground pepper

¾ Tbsp (12 mL) salt (or more to taste)

⅓ cup (80 mL) olive oil

GREEK YOGURT
AND HONEY SNACK

I used to have this snack every day for breakfast when I briefly worked as a lawyer in Cyprus. For me, it is all about excellent-quality honey and yogurt in this dish—if you have those two ingredients you can't really go wrong with any combination of fruit and nuts.

Scoop the yogurt into a small bowl, add the fruit, drizzle with honey and top with a dash of cinnamon and toasted nuts.

Makes 1 serving.

3 large spoonfuls of strained Cypriot or Greek yogurt

fruit of your choice (I prefer bananas or fresh figs)

1 Tbsp (15 mL) excellent-quality honey

dash of cinnamon

1 Tbsp (15 mL) toasted nuts of your choice (I prefer walnuts)

POTATOES WITH RED WINE AND CORIANDER (PATATES ANTINAXTES)

Πατάτες αντιναχτές

I take these potatoes for granted in Cyprus. They are something so normal to me that I never regarded them as "special" or particularly delicious. However, for those who have not had the combination of potato, red wine and dried coriander seeds, it is really quite extraordinary—a fantastic and very Cypriot way to enjoy small potatoes. The name literally translates to "potatoes shaken." Traditionally, one would shake the pot to "crack" open the potatoes after draining the frying oil. Nowadays I find it is easier to just use a kitchen mallet!

2 ⅕ lb (1 kg) baby Yukon Gold potatoes (or any variety of small potatoes)
3 cups (750 mL) vegetable oil, for deep frying
2 Tbsp (30 mL) olive oil
½ cup (125 mL) red wine
2 tsp (10 mL) crushed coriander seeds
salt and pepper, to taste

Wash and dry the potatoes, then crack open with a kitchen mallet. Add the vegetable oil to a frying pan and place over high heat. Once the oil is hot, add the potatoes and cover the frying pan. Deep fry the potatoes until golden brown and cooked throughout.

Remove the potatoes from the oil and place them in a bowl. Drain the vegetable oil from the frying pan. Pour the olive oil into the pan and add the potatoes back in. Pour in the wine and let it evaporate. Add the coriander and salt and pepper, and stir the potatoes for 2 to 3 minutes until done.

Makes 3 to 4 side servings.

EGG LEMON SOUP
WITH MEATBALLS (YOUVARLAKIA)
Γιουβαρλάκια

This soup is very similar to avgolemono soup, but instead of chicken it has meatballs. It feels a bit heartier than avgolemono, and I often make it when I am feeling a bit run-down as it is a heart-warming and comforting soup. What I like most about this soup is that you don't have to have a good chicken broth on hand to make it—the soup will still taste amazing even though you simply start out with water as your base.

MEATBALLS

1 cup (250 mL) finely chopped onion

½ cup (125 mL) finely chopped Italian parsley

1 lb (500 g) ground beef

1 Tbsp (15 mL) olive oil

¾ tsp (4 mL) ground pepper

½ Tbsp (7 mL) salt

1 egg

½ cup (125 mL) rice

SOUP

9 cups (2.25 L) water

1 tsp (5 mL) salt

1 cup (250 mL) cold water

3 eggs

¼ cup (60 mL) freshly squeezed lemon juice (approx. 1 ½ large lemons)

1 cup (250 mL) frozen peas

MEATBALLS

In a bowl, mix together all the ingredients and divide into approximately 34 meatballs. Place to the side.

SOUP

In a large pot, boil the 9 cups (2.25 L) of water together with the salt. Once boiling, add in the meatballs and simmer until the meatballs are cooked. Skim off any froth with a spoon. Check that the rice is cooked inside the meatballs by cutting one in half. Once the meatballs are cooked, lower the heat to a very low simmer, then add 1 cup (250 mL) cold water in order to bring the temperature of the soup down.

In another bowl, beat the eggs with lemon juice until frothy. Slowly add 4 to 5 ladles of hot broth into the egg and lemon mixture, whisking constantly so that the egg mixture does not curdle. Once the egg mixture is about the same temperature as the broth, remove the broth from the heat and pour the egg mixture into the broth and whisk together.

In a small pot, boil the peas until cooked. Strain the peas and add them into the soup.

Makes about 4 to 6 servings.

Main Courses

Main dishes in Cyprus range from simple, seasonal vegetarian dishes to heavy, meat-based dishes, all of which are made with small personal or regional twists. In the majority of Cypriot families, a large meal is still eaten at lunch, with lighter fare enjoyed in the evenings. That is, of course, unless you are going out for dinner at night, in which case dinner is often a late affair starting at about nine o'clock—enough time for one to work up an appetite after lunch!

For me, there is always something to make, cook or inspire me growing in my family's fields or for sale at the local markets. I hope you will find similar inspiration in the pages of this book. Also, a word of thanks here, as I asked people on social media what they might want to see included in a traditional Cypriot cookbook, and have made an effort to include some of these recipes here, including favourites like afelia, anthous and makaronia tou fournou.

FETA AND RICOTTA RAVIOLI (RAVIOLES)

Ραβιόλες

This is one of my favourite Cypriot comfort foods, and I think it's a lot of other people's favourite too. Traditionally, these are made with halloumi, but I love this version which uses feta just as much, if not more. I always make a lot and freeze the extra raviolis, bringing them out when I am in need of something quick and comforting. Serve with lots of grated Anari or Mizithra cheese on top, or pair them with your favourite sauce—you can't go wrong. I have left the cheese measurements in grams because these cheeses often have their weight on the packages, but the cup measurements work as well if you prefer.

Add a pinch of salt to the flour and stir together. On a flat surface, shape your flour mixture into a circle and make a little dip in the centre. Break 3 eggs into the dip. With a fork, begin to beat the eggs with the flour, so that the flour absorbs the eggs. Slowly add warm water to create a firm dough (you may not need all the water). Knead for about 10 minutes until the dough becomes elastic and smooth, then cover with plastic wrap and a towel and let rest for 45 minutes.

Stir together the cheeses, mint, remaining 2 eggs and ½ tsp (2 mL) salt (if needed).

Begin to roll out pieces of the dough until extremely thin. Cut out circular pieces of dough, about 4 inches (10 cm) in diameter. Add 1 tsp (5 mL) of the cheese mixture in the centre. Brush a little water around half the circle's edge. Fold the dough over the cheese mixture and press around the edges with the tines of a fork.

To enjoy the ravioli immediately, boil in hot chicken broth for 5 minutes. Serve with lots of grated Anari on top.

Makes 100 ravioli.

pinch of salt

4 cups (1 L) all-purpose flour

5 large eggs, divided

1 cup (250 mL) warm water (more or less may be needed)

1 ¼ lb (550 g) fresh ricotta (approx. 2 ½ cups/625 mL)

7 oz (200 g) finely grated feta (approx. 1 ¾ cups/430 mL once grated)

1 Tbsp (15 mL) dried mint

½ tsp (2 mL) salt (optional, as the cheeses are salty themselves)

chicken stock, for boiling

salted Anari cheese, grated, for serving (or Mizithra)

SPICY STUFFED ZUCCHINI BLOSSOMS (ANTHOUS)

Ανθούς

This is one of my favourite traditional Cypriot dishes, which is enjoyed by my family every summer and into the early fall while zucchini blossoms are around. Outside of Cyprus I have mostly seen zucchini blossoms fried or stuffed with cheese, and I find that those unfamiliar with Cypriot cuisine are always so excited to discover this recipe. It is a recipe that is extremely popular not only among those familiar with Cypriot foods, but also those who are new to it. It uses a rice stuffing, but does not feel heavy at all. It is a very delicate dish and a special way to make use of summer's bounty.

Place the flowers in a large bowl of cold water (enough to cover them) in order to clean them and remove any green stems. Drain and dry the blossoms. In a bowl, mix together the rice, onion, parsley, mint, basil, tomatoes, pine nuts, pepper, ¼ cup (60 mL) olive oil, salt and cinnamon.

Using a spoon, stuff each flower with about 1 tsp (5 mL) of the mixture, just up to the rim where the blossom opens up so that it fills the opening, leaving a bit of room for the rice to expand (otherwise the blossoms will break). Fold the ends of the petals inward to cover the stuffing.

Drizzle the remaining olive oil on the bottom of a large saucepan. Arrange the flowers in a circular pattern so that they're touching side by side with petals facing out. Once the bottom of the pot is covered, start the second row on top of the first, exactly the same way. It is preferable to use a large pot so that there is only one row of flowers, but two rows is okay as well.

Recipe continued...

50 to 60 zucchini flower blossoms
2 cups (500 mL) long grain rice
1 cup (250 mL) finely chopped onion
½ cup (125 mL) finely chopped parsley
¼ cup (60 mL) finely chopped mint
2 Tbsp (30 mL) finely chopped basil
1 ¼ cups (310 mL) grated tomatoes
⅓ cup (80 mL) pine nuts
½ tsp (2 mL) pepper
½ cup (125 mL) olive oil, divided
2 ½ tsp (12 mL) salt
dash of cinnamon

Once finished arranging the flowers, place a large plate on top of the flowers then pour in the water—it should come up to about half the height of the top row of zucchini flowers. Ensure you add the water after you place the plate on top of the flowers, otherwise the flowers will float to the top. The plate will remain on top of the blossoms for the whole cooking time. Add more water if necessary. Place the saucepan on the stove over medium heat and cover the pot with a lid. Once the liquid begins to boil, turn the heat down to simmer. Cook for about 20 to 25 minutes until most of the liquid has been absorbed, leaving a small space between the lid and the pot for the last 5 minutes.

Makes 6 servings.

ARTICHOKES AND PEAS WITH DILL (ANGINARES ME PIZELI)

Αγκινάρες με μπιζέλι

Every spring I travel with my aunts to our village and gather artichokes from the fields so that there is always a bounty to cook with. I love making this dish, which makes use of all the wonderful spring foods Cyprus has to offer in April and May: fresh dill, lemons and artichokes. This dish uses a lot of oil, but don't be intimidated—it is delicious. It is wonderful as a vegetarian main dish with a piece of bread to soak up the juices.

2 cups (500 mL) water
half a lemon, juiced
2 artichokes
¾ cup (180 mL) olive oil
1 ½ cups (375 mL) chopped green onions
½ cup (125 mL) chopped dill
2 cups (500 mL) frozen peas
salt and pepper, to taste

In a small bowl, add 2 cups (500 mL) water and the juice of half a lemon. Peel, clean and chop each artichoke into 6 small pieces and immediately place into the lemon water so they don't brown.

Add the olive oil to a medium-sized pot and place on medium-high heat on the stove. Once the oil is hot, fry the green onions until soft. Add the artichoke pieces and continue to fry for 2 minutes. Reserve the lemon water. Add the chopped dill, peas and enough lemon water— about 1 scant cup (under 250 mL)—to barely cover the mixture. Cover the pot with a lid and simmer until the artichokes are soft and the water evaporates, about 30 to 40 minutes. Season with salt and pepper towards the end.

Makes 2 servings.

OCTOPUS WINE STEW (XTAPODI KRASATO)

Χταπόδι κρασάτο

I didn't know how to cook octopus when I moved to Cyprus, so I asked my friend Athos if his grandmother—who still cooks for his family often—could teach me. This is Mrs. Angela's recipe. It is easy to make and it's tasty. She prefers to use frozen octopus because it makes the octopus softer once cooked. I prefer to buy it from a fishmonger, because they clean it for me. If you use frozen octopus, don't forget to ensure the octopus is properly cleaned.

¼ cup (60 mL) water

2 lb (900 g) octopus, cleaned and chopped into pieces 2 ½ inches (6 cm) or longer

1 ½ cups (625 mL) grated tomatoes (approx. 2 large tomatoes or 8 oz/225 g)

2 Tbsp (30 mL) tomato paste

¾ tsp (4 mL) sugar

1 cup (250 mL) diced onion (approx. 2 small onions or 5 oz/145 g)

2 ½ Tbsp (37 mL) olive oil

2 ½ Tbsp (37 mL) vegetable oil

half a cinnamon stick (1 ½ inches/4 cm long)

5 cloves

1 bay leaf

¾ cup (180 mL) dry red wine

2 ½ Tbsp (37 mL) red wine or white malt vinegar

salt and pepper, to taste

Fill a large pot with ¼ cup (60 mL) water, add the octopus and place on the stove over medium heat. Boil the octopus with the lid on top for about 30 minutes, until the liquid turns purple. Stir sparingly.

In a small bowl, mix together the grated tomatoes, tomato paste and sugar. Set aside.

Drain and reserve the water from the pot with the octopus. Place the pan with the octopus back onto the stove over medium heat. Add the onion, olive oil, vegetable oil, cinnamon, cloves and bay leaf and lightly fry. Add the red wine, vinegar and tomato mixture.

Once the mixture has begun to boil, reduce to a simmer and add 1 cup (250 mL) of the reserved water from when the octopus was first boiled. Simmer for about 1 hour total, until the liquid is reduced, a nice sauce has formed and the octopus has absorbed the oil and liquid. Add a further 1 cup (250 mL) of the remaining octopus water (or regular water) about halfway through cooking. Season with salt and pepper near the end of cooking as octopus is already quite salty and you may end up adding too much salt if you season the dish before nearing the end.

Makes 3 servings.

FRIED SQUID (KALAMARI)
Καλαμάρι

I always order this dish whenever I go to a fish taverna—I feel that no meal at a fish taverna is complete without it. Certainly no trip to Cyprus is complete without several servings. When making this recipe, try to buy small squid, as they are more true to what people eat in Cyprus. If you buy frozen, defrost and then soak in milk for an hour to make the squid more tender, then pat dry and continue with the recipe below. I always ask the fishmonger to clean the squid for me.

1 lb (500 g) small squid, cleaned and chopped into 2 ½-inch (6 cm) long pieces

olive oil, for frying (enough for a 1-inch/2 ½-cm depth)

all-purpose flour, for dusting

salt and pepper, to taste

freshly squeezed lemon juice, for garnish

salt and pepper, for garnish

dried oregano, for garnish

Clean and chop your squid. Pat the squid well with paper towels to soak up any excess liquid. In a saucepan over high heat, add the oil. Once the oil is hot, toss the squid in flour, ensuring that each piece is well-coated. Add a few pieces of squid at a time to the hot oil and cook for 2 to 3 minutes, until the squid has turned a rosy, light-gold colour.

Use a slotted spoon to remove the squid from the oil and place on paper towels to soak up any excess oil. Serve immediately, garnished with a drizzle of fresh lemon juice, salt and pepper to taste and dried oregano.

Makes 2 servings.

PASTA WITH CHICKEN AND ANARI (MAKARONIA ME ANARI)

Μακαρόνια με αναρή

This is a classic Cypriot comfort food. It is just as simple as it sounds, and the taste is every bit as comforting as you imagine the combination of chicken broth, pasta and salty grated cheese to be. In my family we use half a chicken because there are at least three to four people who will be eating, but you can also make this recipe for just two people by using two chicken thighs.

Boil the chicken in enough salted water to cover until cooked. Once the chicken is cooked, remove and place in a bowl, reserving the broth. Add pasta to the boiling chicken broth and boil until cooked. Remove the pasta and place in a serving bowl.

Before serving, remove and tear the meat from the chicken into small pieces and place in a bowl so that everyone can serve themselves. Divide the pasta between plates—each person can top their pasta with as much chicken and chicken broth as they wish. Liberally squeeze lemon juice over the chicken. Sprinkle a generous amount of grated Anari cheese over the pasta and chicken and enjoy.

Makes 3 to 4 servings.

half a chicken

water, for boiling

salt, to taste

uncooked traditional Cypriot or any other pasta (enough for 3 people)

freshly squeezed lemon juice (about half a lemon per person)

grated salted Anari, as garnish (or Mizithra)

STUFFED VEGETABLES (GEMISTA)
Γεμιστά

I make this every summer, when all the vegetables I need to make it are in season. It feeds a crowd and is delicious. It takes time to prepare, but you always end up with leftovers that are great the next day. I like to use arborio rice as it really soaks up the juices, making each stuffed vegetable even tastier. You can use any combination of vegetables you wish, just ensure that you use at least four tomatoes.

Using a sharp knife, cut the tops off the zucchinis, tomatoes and peppers and scoop out the insides, but do not pierce the skins. Keep the tops to the side. Discard the zucchini and pepper insides, but save the tomato pulp.

Put the tomato pulp in a blender and pulse it to a thick juice. Add the passata, red pepper flakes and sugar to the juice. Season with salt and pepper to taste. Set aside.

Peel the brown skins off of the onions and cut a small wedge lengthwise (from top to bottom) in both. You can discard the wedge. Boil some water in a pot on the stove and cook the onions inside until they become soft. Once soft, turn off the heat and let them sit in the water.

Preheat oven to 325 °F (160 °C).

Heat 4 tsp (20 mL) olive oil in a pan and stirfry the chopped onion, garlic, pine nuts and yellow pepper until the onions are softened. Add half of the tomato mixture, bring to a boil and stir in the rice. Add more salt and pepper if necessary. Cook for about 10 to 12 minutes, until the rice starts absorbing the liquid. Add more water from the pot in which the onions were boiled if the mixture gets dry.

Recipe continued...

2 small zucchinis

4 juicy, ripe tomatoes

2 large peppers (any colour)

2 cups (500 mL) tomato passata

1 tsp (5 mL) crushed red pepper flakes

1 tsp (5 mL) sugar + extra for sprinkling

salt and pepper, to taste

2 onions + 1 finely chopped small onion

½ cup (125 mL) olive oil, divided

3 garlic cloves, finely diced

½ cup (125 mL) pine nuts

3 Tbsp (45 mL) chopped yellow pepper

1 cup (250 mL) arborio rice

3 Tbsp (45 mL) flat-leaf parsley, chopped

1 ½ Tbsp (22 mL) butter, in little pieces

spoonful of creamy yogurt, for serving

Remove pot from heat and stir in the parsley. Sprinkle the insides of the tomatoes, zucchini and peppers with salt. Fill each tomato, pepper and zucchini about two-thirds full with the rice mixture and put their tops back on. Take the boiled onions and carefully peel each layer off. Scoop some of the mixture into each onion layer, then wrap the skin around the filling to keep it tight.

Arrange the vegetables in a large ovenproof dish about 8 to 12 inches (20 to 30 cm) in diameter. Gently add about 2 cups (500 mL) of the remaining tomato sauce and water from the pot in which the onions were boiled to the bottom of the pan around the vegetables. Add 1 tsp (5 mL) liquid on top of the rice in the vegetables.

Drizzle the remaining olive oil overtop the vegetables and sprinkle with a little salt. Sprinkle a little sugar on top of the tomatoes. Dot the butter on the vegetables. Cook for 1 ½ hours, until the vegetables are soft and have begun to brown on top and there is a little thickened sauce on the bottom of the pan. Turn up the heat to 350 °F (175 °C) or 375 °F (190 °C) for the last 20 minutes if you would like the vegetables to crisp on top. Be sure to baste the vegetables 3 or 4 times while cooking, and add a little more onion water if the sauce becomes too dry. Serve with a dollop of creamy yogurt.

Makes 12 to 15 stuffed vegetables.

CYPRIOT LASAGNA (MAKARONIA TOU FOURNOU)

Μακαρόνια του φούρνου

At every large celebratory gathering in Cyprus there is a big dish of makaronia tou fournou, the Cypriot version of lasagna. You may know this recipe as "pastitsio," which is the Greek name for it. The Cypriot version is slightly different from the Greek: my mom's Greek friend will add tomato to the meat sauce, and she uses beef instead of pork. The Cypriot makaronia tou fournou is also creamier than pastitsio. In our household, my aunt is the "maker" of the makaronia tou fournou, and this is her recipe.

PASTA

12 cups (3 L) water
2 chicken bouillon cubes
1 Tbsp (15 mL) salt (optional)
1 lb (500 g) Mezzani "A" pasta
2 Tbsp (30 mL) salted butter, for coating the pasta
½ cup (125 mL) grated Anari (or Mizithra)

FILLING

3 Tbsp (45 mL) olive oil
¾ cup (180 mL) diced onion
1 ⅓ lb (600 g) minced pork
1 tsp (5 mL) salt
¼ tsp (1 mL) pepper
½ tsp (2 mL) cinnamon
¼ cup (60 mL) diced parsley

Ingredients continued…

PASTA

Fill a pot with 12 cups (3 L) water and mix in the chicken bouillon cubes and salt (if desired). Boil and cook the pasta until al dente, then drain. Place the pasta back into the pot and mix in the salted butter and grated Anari. Set aside.

FILLING

In a large pan over high heat, warm the olive oil. Sauté the onions until translucent then add the minced meat, salt, pepper and cinnamon. Once the minced meat is cooked, add in the parsley and cook for another minute. Remove from the stove and drain the mixture so that no liquid is left in the meat sauce. Set aside.

BÉCHAMEL SAUCE

Heat the milk so that it is hot but not boiling. Add the olive oil to a large pot and heat it. Add the flour all at once and stir it around until cooked. Add the milk, a little bit at a time, until all the milk has been added, whisking constantly. Bring the béchamel sauce to a boil until it bubbles. Remove the pot from the heat, whisk in the Anari, bouillon cube and salt and continue stirring until both have been incorporated. Add the egg yolks one at a time and whisk until fully incorporated.

Recipe continued…

BÉCHAMEL SAUCE

5 cups (1.25 L) milk

½ cup (125 mL) olive oil

10 Tbsp (150 mL) traditional Cypriot "village flour" (or bread flour)

1 cup (250 mL) grated Anari (or Mizithra)

1 chicken bouillon cube

1 tsp (5 mL) salt

2 large egg yolks, beaten

2 ½ Tbsp (37 mL) breadcrumbs, divided

½ tsp (2 mL) cinnamon

1 ½ Tbsp (22 mL) grated Anari (or Mizithra)

ASSEMBLY

Preheat oven to 350 °F (175 °C). Sprinkle 1 Tbsp (15 mL) breadcrumbs onto the bottom of a 13- × 10-inch (33 × 25 cm) Pyrex dish or casserole pan. Place half the pasta on the bottom of the dish followed by all of the meat sauce then a thin layer of béchamel sauce. Add the remaining pasta and béchamel sauce. Mix together the remaining breadcrumbs, cinnamon and 1 ½ Tbsp (22 mL) grated Anari, and sprinkle overtop.

Bake in the oven for 50 minutes Once baked, remove from the oven and let cool for 1 hour before serving, so that the béchamel sauce cools and thickens.

Makes 12 servings.

RABBIT ONION STEW (KOUNELI STIFADO)
Κουνέλι στιφάδο

For the longest time my mom told us that this dish was made with chicken—I believed this right into my twenties. In fact, when I was 24 I insisted to my cousin that my mom made her stifado differently—with chicken, not rabbit. I was wrong; it was just my mom's technique to make sure her kids ate their dinner. This is my friend Antoni's recipe—it was the first recipe I made when settling into a new flat, and it immediately brought warmth to my new home. It's excellent. You can usually find rabbit in your local butchers shop.

¼ cup (60 mL) olive oil, for frying, divided

1 whole rabbit, chopped into pieces, head and innards removed (approx. 1 ⅔ lb/750 g)

35 banana shallots, peeled but left whole

1 cinnamon stick

1 heaped tsp (5+ mL) whole peppercorns

dash dried cumin

2 cups (500 mL) red wine

¼ cup (60 mL) red wine vinegar

2 Tbsp (30 mL) tomato paste

3 bay leaves

1 cup (250 mL) water

salt and pepper, to taste

pasta and grated Anari or Mizithra, to serve alongside

Heat 3 Tbsp (45 mL) olive oil in a large pot over the stove. Add the rabbit and lightly brown the pieces on each side, then remove and place these pieces on a plate.

Add 1 Tbsp (15 mL) olive oil to the same pot. Add the shallots. Once the shallots are lightly browned, add the rabbit, cinnamon, peppercorns, cumin, wine, vinegar, tomato paste, bay leaves and water. Close the lid, leaving a slight gap, and bring to a boil. Once the stew reaches a boil, reduce the temperature to a simmer and cook for about 1 hour, until the meat falls off the bones and the juices have reduced into a nice sauce.

Serve with pasta and grated Anari or Mizithra cheese sprinkled on top.

Makes 4 servings.

FRESH BLACK-EYED PEAS WITH TUNA (LOUVIA)

Λουβιά

This is a typical daily meal in Cyprus in the summertime that's very light and healthy. It is often served with tuna and pickles. If you cannot find fresh black-eyed peas, you can also make this recipe with dried black-eyed peas and chopped fresh Swiss chard (to replace the zucchini). In this case the same method applies as below, simply cook the dried peas a bit longer before adding the Swiss chard.

Clean the fresh black-eyed beans by removing the tops and tail ends. If the beans are very green, simply snap them into smaller pieces about 2 ½ inches (6 cm) long. If the beans are light green, discard the shells and remove and reserve the beans. It does not matter what proportion of shelled and unshelled peas you end up with, though I prefer more unshelled pieces than shelled.

Bring a large pot of water to a boil on the stove. Add the fresh black-eyed peas, cover with a lid and cook on medium-high heat for 20 minutes.

Add the zucchini pieces and boil together until the zucchini is cooked, about another 10 to 15 minutes.

Once cooked, turn off heat and squeeze the juice of half a lemon into the water. Let sit until ready to eat. Before serving, drain the water.

In a bowl, add the tuna, parsley, green onions, celery, pickles, olive oil, lemon juice and salt in a bowl and mix together. Set aside.

Dress each serving of black-eyed peas with a drizzle of olive oil and a generous squeeze of lemon. Salt to taste and add a few spoonfuls of the tuna and pickle mixture.

Makes 3 servings.

FRESH BLACK-EYED PEAS

1 ⅔ lb (750 g) fresh black-eyed beans (yielding about ¾ lb/350 g unshelled beans and 5 oz/150 g shelled peas)

11 ½ oz (325 g) glyko (sweet) zucchini, chopped ¾ inch (2 cm) thick into semicircular pieces and deseeded

juice of ½ lemon

TUNA SIDE DISH

1 can tuna, tinned juices drained (approx. 5 ½ oz/160 g)

3 Tbsp (45 mL) parsley, finely chopped

⅓ cup (80 mL) finely diced green onions

¼ cup (60 mL) finely diced celery

2 Tbsp (30 mL) finely chopped pickles

3 Tbsp (45 mL) olive oil

3 Tbsp (45 mL) freshly squeezed lemon juice

salt, to taste

juice of ½ to 1 fresh lemon, to taste

olive oil, to taste

salt, to taste

CYPRIOT LENTILS (FAKES)
Φακές

This dish is made often in Cypriot homes. It's an easy and tasty dish, and ideal for those fasting for religious reasons. This is frequently the meal I turn to when I am late arriving home and want a warm but easy-to-prepare meal. Note to the cook: I do add more onions than the traditional recipe calls for, because it is my favourite part. Cut all the onions the same size, otherwise some will burn. Do not overcook the lentils and rice or they will become mushy. If you wish to add more onions, feel free to do so, but you will also need to increase the amount of oil in which they are fried. You can't really go wrong with the amount of onions you add, it is just a matter of personal taste. This dish is best enjoyed with a dollop of creamy Greek yogurt.

3 ½ Tbsp (52 mL) olive oil, divided
2 small onions, sliced equally into
　　¼-inch (5 mm) thick rings and
　　halved into semi-circles (approx.
　　6 oz/180 g)
½ cup (125 mL) small green lentils
2 ½ cups (625 mL) water
¼ cup (60 mL) parboiled rice
salt and pepper, to taste
Greek yogurt or feta cheese, to serve
　　alongside

Pour 2 ½ Tbsp (37 mL) oil into a large frying pan over medium-high heat and add onions. Fry the onions for about 15 to 20 minutes until soft, browned and beginning to caramelize. Stir frequently. Do not let them burn. You should be able to easily cut through the onions with a wooden spoon. Turn off the heat and let the onions sit in the pan.

While the onions are frying, place the lentils, 1 ½ cups (375 mL) water and the remaining 1 Tbsp (15 mL) olive oil into a saucepan over medium heat on the stove. Cover the pot with a lid, leaving a slight gap for air to escape. Cook for about 10 minutes, until the lentils are half cooked, then add the rice, the remaining 1 cup (250 mL) water and salt to taste and replace the lid. Stir occasionally to prevent the rice from sticking. Add more water if needed, but not too much, as you eventually want all the water to evaporate.

Cook the lentils and rice mixture for about 10 to 15 minutes until cooked but still firm. Turn off the heat, leave the lid on the pot and let the lentils and rice continue to cook inside for another 5 minutes, absorbing any remaining liquid. Mix together all of the onions and lentils. Serve with spoonfuls of Greek yogurt and/or pieces of feta cheese.

Makes 2 servings.

PORK MEATBALLS (KEFTEDES)
Κεφτέδες

When in Cyprus, I often ask people what their favourite meal is. Most of them say it's their mother's fried pork meatballs (keftedes) served alongside pourgouri (p. 107) and a generous helping of yogurt. The combination never disappoints. It is one of my favourite childhood dinners, and remains one of my favourite comfort meals to this day.

½ lb (250 g) ground pork
½ lb (250 g) ground beef
¾ cup (180 mL) finely chopped onion
½ cup (125 mL) finely chopped parsley
2 potatoes (should measure 9 oz/260 g after having been peeled), finely grated, water squeezed out
2 eggs
¼ cup (60 mL) breadcrumbs
2 Tbsp (30 mL) olive oil
2 ½ tsp (12 mL) dried mint
¼ tsp (1 mL) ground pepper
¾ tsp (4 mL) salt, or less to taste
dash of cinnamon
2 cups (500 mL) olive oil, for frying

Place all ingredients in a large bowl except for the frying oil and mix together well. Form into little oval balls about 1 ¼ × 2 ½ inches (3 × 6 cm).

Add the frying oil to a large pot over high heat. Once the oil is hot, add enough meatballs to cover the bottom. Leave them for at least 2 minutes, then begin turning them as they cook, until golden brown. It should take about 6 to 7 minutes to cook the meatballs. Remove once cooked and place on paper towels to absorb any excess oil. Repeat until all meatballs are cooked.

Makes 30 to 35 meatballs.

ZUCCHINI PATTIES (KOLOKYTHOKEFTEDES)
Κολοκυθοκεφτέδες

This dish is typically enjoyed in the summertime when there are lots of zucchini available. Zucchinis are usually served alongside yogurt, and some pourgouri (see p. 107). In my family we think of them like the vegetarian version of keftedes (see p. 156). I have written this recipe so that those outside of Cyprus can easily make it. However, you can easily substitute the cheeses out for whatever your preference is (e.g., halloumi and salted Anari cheese for feta and kefalotyri, and parmesan for Pecorino Romano).

Preheat an oven broiler to 485 °F (250 °C). Lightly sauté the onion in 3 Tbsp (45 mL) olive oil until translucent.

Sprinkle a little salt on top of the zucchini and strain for at least 10 minutes. Squeeze the water out of the zucchini and place zucchini in a large bowl.

Add the onion and the rest of the ingredients (except for the breadcrumbs) to the bowl and mix together. Shape the zucchini mixture into circular patties approximately ½ × 4 inches (1 × 10 cm). Coat all the patties with breadcrumbs, ensuring they are covered with breadcrumbs on all sides.

Put patties onto a baking tray covered in parchment paper, drizzle with a little olive oil and place under the broiler for 20 minutes until golden brown. Turn all the patties and cook for another 10 minutes.

Makes 12 large patties.

1 cup (250 mL) finely diced onion
3 Tbsp (45 mL) olive oil + extra for drizzling
6 cups (1.4 L) grated zucchini
½ cup (125 mL) chopped parsley
2 Tbsp (30 mL) chopped mint
2 Tbsp (30 mL) chopped dill
1 Tbsp (15 mL) chopped basil
3 Tbsp (45 mL) breadcrumbs
2 eggs
1 cup (250 mL) grated feta cheese
½ cup (125 mL) grated kefalotyri
¼ cup (60 mL) Pecorino Romano
salt and pepper, to taste
1 cup (250 mL) breadcrumbs, for coating

CYPRIOT SOUVLAKI (SOUVLAKI)
Σουβλάκι

Cypriot souvlaki is different from traditional Greek souvlaki. In Cyprus, the pita bread is larger and thinner, and is filled to the brim with salad, with an option to add a yellow pickle or talatouri (in Greece they call it tzatziki) on top. There is also the option to ask for a "mixed" souvlaki in Cyprus, which includes a Cypriot sausage called sheftalia—pork encased in caul fat. These are delicious, but a little difficult to make, so I haven't included the recipe in this book. This souvlaki recipe is the one I turn to when I am outside of Cyprus craving souvlaki. In Cyprus, the meat is always cooked on a grill. You can do this if you wish—simply skewer the chicken pieces before placing them on the grill. Mostly though, I simply fry the meat instead of grilling it—it's just as tasty and easier to make.

Place the chicken pieces in a bowl with the garlic, onion, olive oil and oregano, and let it marinate for 30 minutes to 1 hour.

Salt the chicken before frying it. Cook the chicken in a frying pan over medium-high heat until cooked through.

Serve in a toasted pita bread with diced cabbage, tomato, cucumber and parsley, all drizzled in lemon juice, with a dollop of Cucumber, Garlic and Mint Dip if you wish.

Makes 2 to 4 servings, depending on how much meat you like in each souvlaki.

1 skinless chicken breast and 1 chicken thigh (approx. 1 lb/470 g; you can also omit the chicken thigh and just use 1 lb/470 g of chicken breast), chopped into 1-inch (2.5 cm) pieces

3 garlic cloves, sliced

1 small onion, sliced

3 Tbsp (45 mL) olive oil

1 tsp (5 mL) dried oregano

¾ tsp (4 mL) salt

ground pepper, to taste

1 to 2 large pita breads, toasted

diced cabbage, for serving

diced tomato, for serving

diced cucumber, for serving

diced parsley, for serving

freshly squeezed lemon, for serving

Cucumber, Garlic and Mint Dip (p. 174), for serving (optional)

PORK IN RED WINE AND CORIANDER (AFELIA)

Αφέλια

This is a hearty and warm dish—the type of dish I would expect to enjoy when exploring the mountain villages of Cyprus in the winter. It is often paired with a type of pilaf, either the plain and simple version (which is simply a mixture of rice and vermicelli pasta) or the Tomato Bulgur Wheat Pilaf on page 107, or you can just enjoy it on its own since I have added potatoes into this recipe as well. My mom would make this for us on a regular basis growing up, and it is still very popular in Cyprus (I often have people asking me for a recipe). Note that my mom and I use pork tenderloin when making this recipe, but traditionally boneless pork meat from the neck or shoulder is used, which actually results in a more tender dish.

MARINADE

1 ½ cups (375 mL) dry wine (enough to cover the meat)

2 tsp (10 mL) crushed coriander seeds

½ tsp (2 mL) black pepper

AFELIA

1 lb (450 g) pork tenderloin or boneless pork shoulder or neck, cut into cubes that are just larger than bite-sized

⅓ cup (80 mL) vegetable oil, for frying

8 fingerling potatoes, cut lengthwise (just over 2 cups/500 mL) if measuring once cut

⅓ cup (80 mL) red wine

½ cup (125 mL) water

1 Tbsp (15 mL) crushed coriander seeds

1 tsp (5 mL) salt

¼ tsp (1 mL) pepper

Mix together the marinade ingredients. Marinate the pork in the marinade for at least 3 hours or overnight.

Add the vegetable oil to a large frying pan over high heat on the stove. Once the oil is hot, brown the potatoes in the oil on all sides, then remove and set aside. Remove pan from heat and drain half the oil. Place pan back on heat and brown the pork on all sides, reserving the marinade.

Once pork is browned, add ½ cup (250 mL) marinade and the red wine. Cook for 5 minutes, then add the water, coriander seeds, salt and pepper and reduce heat to a simmer. Cover with a lid and simmer for 35 minutes.

After 35 minutes, open the lid for 10 minutes so that the liquid begins to evaporate and create a nice sauce. Continue to simmer until the meat is tender and potatoes are soft and there is just a little liquid left.

Makes 3 to 4 servings.

LAMB ORZO STEW (KRITHARAKI ME ARNI)
Κριθαράκι με αρνί

This is an extremely warm and comforting food that I enjoy making in the winter time. It is also a great dish to make for a small dinner crowd. You only need one big pot, and it is really simple to make even though the taste of lamb falling off the bone would have you and any guest believing it was more difficult. We make kritharaki with lamb in my family, but if you wish to use chicken thighs you can make this substitution. I would add that I never feel this meal is complete without a generous topping of salted Anari cheese or Mizithra, so ensure you have some on hand.

¼ cup (60 mL) olive oil, divided
2 lamb shanks
1 small onion
1 large garlic clove
5 cups (1.25 L) blended fresh tomatoes (skin off, tough bits removed before blending)
3 Tbsp (45 mL) diced parsley
2 Tbsp (30 mL) diced basil
pinch of sugar
½ Tbsp (7 mL) salt
pepper, to taste
1 cinnamon stick
1 bay leaf
8 oz (225 g) orzo pasta
salted Anari or Mizithra cheese, grated, for serving

In a large pot over medium-high heat, add the oil and lamb shanks and brown on all sides (there should be a sizzling sound when you add the lamb into the pot; if there isn't, the oil is not hot enough). Once the lamb is browned, remove the lamb shanks and set aside.

In the same pot, still over medium-high heat, fry the onion and garlic until soft but not burnt. Add in the tomatoes, parsley, basil, sugar, salt and pepper. Stir for 1 minute. Add the lamb shanks back in with the cinnamon stick and bay leaf. Turn the heat down and simmer for 1 hour. Check if the lamb has become tender by using a fork to try to pull the meat off the bone. If the meat easily separates from the bone it is ready. The lamb shanks may need up to 1 ½ hours to become tender, in which case you may need to add a little more water to the sauce.

Once the lamb is tender, add in the orzo pasta and cook until done. Add more water if necessary to ensure that the liquid stays saucy. Serve with grated Anari cheese or Mizithra on top.

Makes 4 servings.

Pickles, Dips & Extras

Please do not think that because this section is an "extras" section it is any less important than the others. I cannot overstate the importance of the recipes in this section to Cypriot cuisine, some of which I am always asked about in my blog. Simply put, the recipes are so unique that I felt they deserved to have their own section rather than be awkwardly filed into another.

In Cyprus, there is always something on the kitchen table inviting you to sit down and nibble. Similarly, there is always something delightful tucked away in jars or bottles in the cupboard, waiting to be spread or used in a recipe. These are some of those foods.

ORANGE BLOSSOM WATER (ANTHONERO)

Ανθόνερο

Visitors to Cyprus will tell you it has a distinctive smell. Over the years, I have come to realize that during the spring, this smell is the scent of orange blossoms, which always seem to float around in the air. It is such a beautiful aroma, and one that is possible to bottle if you know how to make orange blossom water. In fact, we still have a bottle of my great-aunt's homemade orange blossom water she made from over 10 years ago in our fridge in Canada, and it takes me back to Cyprus as soon as I open it.

It is best to collect the orange blossoms in the early morning, while they are most fragrant and the sun has not touched them. I have included this recipe for preservation, rather than for reproduction. If you wish to make it, I would recommend trying to find someone who can show you the steps. You can find orange blossom water in most speciality Mediterranean or Middle Eastern grocery stores, and that is the easiest way to get a hold of some. There are a couple of recipes in here that make use of orange blossom water, namely, Honey Cinnamon Sticks (p. 65) and Auntie Maroulla's Peach and Orange Blossom Trifle (p. 238). In this recipe, I used an old-fashioned distiller, where one adds the water into a base that is heated over a gas stove.

Follow the distiller instructions and place it over the lowest heat setting. Add the orange blossoms and leaves. After 20 minutes, orange blossom water will drip out of the distiller's tap. Catch the orange blossom water in a sterilized bottle. Continue this process until you have about 3 cups (750 mL) of orange blossom water. Do not let the process go on longer, as the orange blossom water will become less fragrant.

Close and store your bottle in a sunny location for 2 days. Then, store the bottle in a dark cupboard until needed. Do not worry if the orange blossom water does not immediately smell the way you expect it to, the scent will strengthen with time.

11 cups (2.6 L) Seville orange
   blossoms
3 young Seville orange leaves
7 cups (1.75 L) water

Makes 3 cups (750 mL).

PICKLED CAPER SHOOTS (KAPARI)

Κάππαρη

In the springtime, I will venture with my family to the mountains to forage for baby caper shoots. Capers like to grow in the cracks of steep cliffs, and it is often a sight to behold as I crane off the edge of a cliff, clinging to my grandma's cane with my aunts on the other end. The end result: pickled baby caper shoots that add a punch of flavour to salads and main courses. In most countries, I have only seen pickled caper buds for sale, but I think baby caper shoots are better than the buds! I have included this recipe for preservation purposes, as it would be difficult to reproduce. If interested in pickling your own, I recommend learning from someone who has made these before, otherwise it is possible to buy them from most grocery stores in Cyprus.

Place the caper stems in an unsealed glass jar and cover them with water. Cover the jar with a cloth. Store in a dark place for 4 days. On the 4th day, empty the water from the jar and refill with enough water to cover the stems. Recover with a cloth and store for another 4 days, until the caper stems become dark green in colour.

On the 8th day from when the capers were first put into water, remove the caper stems and rinse them well with water. Generously sprinkle the stems with salt accordingly and let them rest in a strainer for 10 minutes. Place the stems in a bottle, cover them with vinegar and seal the jar. When serving alongside salad, drizzle olive oil over the stems.

Makes as much as you gather.

baby caper shoots, thorns removed (stems should be 4 to 6 inches/10 to 15 cm long)

1 heaped tsp (5+ mL) salt for every 7 caper stems

water, for washing

red wine vinegar (enough to cover the pickled capers)

CUCUMBER, GARLIC AND MINT DIP (TALATOURI)

Ταλατούρι

There are so many dips in Cyprus, I had a hard time choosing which one to include. In the end, I chose two dips (for the other, see p. 180). This is the one I make the most. In Cyprus, it is known as talatouri, but you may know it by its more common Greek name "tzatziki." The main difference between the Greek version and the Cypriot version of this dip is that in Cyprus we add mint instead of dill as the herb. There are a few recipes that use it in this book, and I find it is also nice to simply make it in order to enjoy alongside fresh vegetables.

1 cup (250 mL) finely grated cucumber
¾ tsp (4 mL) salt, divided
3 garlic cloves, grated
(approx. ½ tsp/2 mL once grated)
1 Tbsp (15 mL) olive oil
2 cups (500 mL) strained Greek yogurt
1 tsp (5 mL) dried mint
1 Tbsp (15 mL) lemon juice
⅛ tsp (0.5 mL) pepper, to taste

Place the grated cucumber in a strainer and sprinkle with a ¼ tsp (1 mL) salt. Leave for 15 minutes, then squeeze out any excess water.

Place the garlic and olive oil in a medium-sized bowl. Add the yogurt, cucumber, mint, lemon juice and ½ tsp (2 mL) salt and pepper. Mix together well. If the mixture appears runny, add a touch more yogurt. Serve alongside bread.

Makes 4 to 6 servings as a starter.

CORIANDER
SMASHED OLIVES (ELIES TSAKISTES)
Ελιές τσακιστές

In the fall, the olive trees become heavy, laden with large green olives. Just before they begin to brown, we gather the biggest, fleshiest olives (from the variety of olive trees indigenous to Cyprus). We literally sit on my aunt's veranda, take rocks and smash the olives to crack them open, ensuring not to crack the pit. This is where the name of this recipe—which translates to "crushed" olives—comes from.

This is an extremely popular olive recipe all over Cyprus, and you will usually find a little bowl of these sitting on a kitchen table or on a table at a Cypriot taverna. I don't feel like it is a complete Cypriot meal without enjoying some of these at the start. I have included this recipe mostly for preservation purposes, and would recommend learning to make these from someone who knows how, or buying them from Cyprus, as preparation can be a bit tricky.

1 heaped cup (250+ mL) fresh green olives (gathered in October in Cyprus, just before the olives brown)

water, for curing

BRINE

¼ cup (60 mL) salt

2 cups (500 mL) water

2 Tbsp (30 mL) lemon juice

olive oil (enough to cover the olives)

DRESSING

2 cloves garlic, finely chopped

2 tsp (10 mL) lemon juice

1 tsp (5 mL) crushed dried coriander seeds

2 tsp (10 mL) olive oil

1 thin slice of lemon, chopped into little pieces

Take the green olives and crack them open using a rock or kitchen mallet. Do not crack the pits of the olives. Put the cracked olives in a jar, fill with water and close the top. Leave for 8 days, changing the water every 2 days (so that the bitterness leaves the olives). On the 9th day, rinse the olives well with water.

BRINE

In a separate jar, add the salt, water and lemon juice, and stir until dissolved. Place the olives in a different jar, removing any that appear mushy and bruised. Pour olive oil over the olives and add the brine. After 1 week, the olives are ready to eat. Remove 1 cup (250 mL) olives with a slotted spoon from the brine, rinse with water and place in a little bowl.

DRESSING

Add the dressing ingredients together in a bowl, stir and serve.

Makes 1 heaped cup (250+ mL) olives.

MEDITERRANEAN MEDLAR JAM (MARMALADE MOSPHILO)

Μαρμελάδα μόσφιλο

I often like to ask people in Cyprus what their favourite Cypriot food is. I have heard "mosphilo" so many times that I decided I had to make it for myself and, having now tried it, I can understand why it is so popular. It reminds me of caramel, apple and sweet-scented geranium flavours all mixed together. In the fall you can find the tree that produces mosphilo berries laden with yellow berries. They never last long on the trees, however. My aunts, as well as countless others around the island, quickly pick them to make this special jelly, which is essentially a jam. If lucky, I sometimes find buckets of these berries at my local market and will buy a bucket or two, much to the delight of my aunt with whom I always make this jelly. It also takes a prized position in our jam cupboard in Canada, eaten on special occasions so that it can last us throughout the year.

In a large saucepan over the stove, bring the water to a boil and add the mosphila. Simmer for 2 hours, ensuring to press the mosphila as they are boiling, to release the juices and pectin inside. Reduce the liquid to 6 cups (1.4 L), then remove and discard the mosphila with a slotted spoon.

Pour the liquid into a bowl through a fine strainer. Pour the strained liquid back into the saucepan and add the sugar, lemon juice and sweet geranium leaves. Place the saucepan on the stove and bring to a boil, then simmer, stirring occasionally, to ensure the sugar melts. After 10 minutes, remove the rose-scented geranium leaves.

Simmer for about 45 minutes until the setting point is reached. You can test the setting point using your preferred method, but my aunt and I simply look to see if the jelly is slowly dripping off the spoon, with lots of tiny bubbles forming on top of the simmering jelly after 45 minutes. Remove from heat and leave for 1 to 2 minutes to cool. Pour into sterilized jam jars. Leave to cool and seal jam jars with a lid.

Makes as much as you like.

20 cups (4.75 L) water

2 ⅕ lb (1 kg) mosphila (species of hawthorn more commonly known as "azarole" or the Mediterranean "medlar")

6 cups (1.4 L) sugar

7 tsp (35 mL) lemon juice

2 to 3 large rose-scented geranium leaves (approx. 1 ½ × 2 inches/ 4 × 5 cm)

TAHINI–GARLIC DIP (TASHI)

Τασιή

This is my other favourite Cypriot dip that I enjoy making. Every time I order kalamari I have a bowl of this on the table to pair it with. It is a tangy, savoury dip that pairs beautifully with bread, particularly koulouria. I also think it would be tasty over vegetables or rice, if you were so inclined. I have ensured that the consistency of the dip is thick and reminiscent of my favourite fish taverna in Cyprus, but if you find the dip is too runny for your taste, simply add more tahini. You can also add more garlic if you wish, but I would only do so after trying the recipe below first.

½ cup (125 mL) tahini
⅓ cup (80 mL) lemon juice
1 regular-sized garlic clove, minced
(approx. 1 tsp/5 mL once minced)
¾ tsp (4 mL) salt
¼ cup (60 mL) water
3 Tbsp (45 mL) olive oil

Place all ingredients in a food processor, or use a handheld immersion blender to mix everything together on high speed.

Makes 1 large bowl of tashi, enough for 3 to 4 people.

Cakes & Sweets

In Cyprus, it is very common at the end of a meal to simply enjoy whatever seasonal fruit is on hand: sweet watermelon in the summer, juicy clementines in the winter, pink and red pomegranates in the fall and local strawberries for a very short period in the spring. Having said that, there is always a large variety of traditional sweets and cakes available for those who want a sweet bite, usually offered alongside an afternoon coffee or after a large meal. Some desserts I enjoy making only when the occasion calls for it, others I make all year around.

I have a sweet tooth so it was difficult to narrow this section down. These are some of my favourites—both traditional and modern. All are recipes that my family makes in Cyprus.

AUNTIE EVRI'S HALLOUMI MINT BUNDT CAKE (HALLOUMOPITA)

Χαλουμόπιτα

The combination of halloumi and mint is so good that I often find myself thinking of new ways to combine the two. My aunt has been using this combination in a sweet tea cake she makes that the whole family loves. It is usually on offer for guests, and at large casual gatherings. I always found the recipe a bit unusual, but there is never any cake left, so it definitely works!

Grease and flour a Bundt pan 8 ½ inches (22 cm) in diameter and preheat oven to 325 °F (160 °C).

Beat the egg whites until medium peaks form.

In a medium bowl, mix the baking powder and flour. In another large bowl, mix the egg yolks and sunflower oil for 2 minutes. Begin adding the flour, then milk and finally the beaten egg whites. Add the cheeses and mint at the end.

Pour the batter into the Bundt pan. Bake the Bundt cake for about 50 minutes to 1 hour, until a knife inserted comes out clean.

Makes 1 large Bundt cake (about 20 to 25 slices).

3 cups (750 mL) all-purpose flour (approx.) + extra for the pan

5 eggs, separated into egg whites and egg yolks

1 Tbsp (15 mL) baking powder

1 cup (250 mL) sunflower oil

1 cup (250 mL) milk

⅔ cup (160 mL) grated kefalotyri cheese

1 ¼ cups (310 mL) grated halloumi

1 heaped Tbsp (15+ mL) dried mint

MRS. POPI'S PISTACHIO BAKLAVA (BAKLAVA)

Μπακλαβάς

I am extremely picky with my baklava. I don't like it too sweet. It has to have a buttery flavour with a touch of sweetness and a crispy phyllo. In Cyprus we call baklava made with pistachios (rather than almonds) "Lebanese-style" baklava, because most baklava in Cyprus is made with almonds and cinnamon. This recipe was kindly given to me by Mrs. Popi Mina, who makes the best baklava I have ever tried. You can substitute clarified unsalted butter for unsalted butter if you prefer, but using non-clarified butter is easier. This baklava is just the right amount of sweet, buttery and flaky. It's perfect. It is really important that you have the right-sized pan for the dish, as it ensures that the ratio of butter and sweetness per piece is just perfect.

SYRUP

1 ½ cups (375 mL) water
1 ½ cups (375 mL) sugar
rind from a whole lemon
2 tsp (10 mL) freshly squeezed lemon juice
6 Tbsp (90 mL) honey

BAKLAVA

2 cups (500 mL) unsalted shelled pistachios, roughly chopped after measuring
32 sheets phyllo (each sheet about 9 × 12 inches/23 × 30 cm)
½ lb (250 g) unsalted butter
½ Tbsp (7 mL) water
1 Tbsp (15 mL) unsalted shelled pistachios, roughly chopped, for garnish

SYRUP

In a small saucepan over high heat, heat the water, sugar, lemon rind, lemon juice and honey. Bring to a boil then let simmer. Skim any foam off the top as it heats. Continue to simmer until the syrup becomes glossy and slightly thickens, about 20 minutes—the liquid should drip from the spoon in one continuous drip. Place it to the side to cool. Ensure that the syrup has cooled completely before making the baklava.

BAKLAVA

Preheat oven to 340 °F (170 °C). Divide the pistachios into 5 portions. Place 6 sheets of phyllo on the bottom of a 9- × 12-inch (23 × 30 cm) Pyrex pan that is 1 ½ inches (4 cm) deep. Place a layer of pistachios on top, sprinkling some in the corners. Place 5 more sheets of phyllo on top, along with another layer of pistachios. Repeat this step 3 times. Place 6 sheets of phyllo on top as a final step. With a pizza slicer or sharp knife, slice the baklava into 49 little rectangles about 1 ¼ × 1 ½ inches (3 × 4 cm) each.

Recipe continued...

In a small saucepan, heat the butter until it has melted and pour it all over the baklava, ensuring it gets into all the cracks. Generously sprinkle ½ Tbsp (7 mL) water over the baklava before placing it in the oven.

Bake for 20 minutes at 340 °F (170 °C), then reduce the temperature to 325 °F (160 °C) and bake for 20 minutes. Reduce temperature again to 190 °F (90 °C) and cook 35 to 40 minutes, turning the baklava pan so that all sides are evenly cooked. Cover the top with tinfoil at any stage if the baklava looks like it may burn. The baklava is done when there appears to be very little buttery liquid left in the bottom of the dish and the tops are a nice golden brown.

Immediately pour the cooled syrup all over the hot baklava. Sprinkle with ground pistachio nuts and serve.

Makes about 49 small pieces of baklava.

ALMOND MACAROONS (ERGOLAVI)
Εργολάβοι

These cookies have a crunchy, nutty, almond exterior and a soft and chewy center that tastes like marzipan. In Cyprus, these are traditionally handed out as gifts to guests at a child's baptism. However, these cookies are good enough to be made and enjoyed without an occasion for celebration in my opinion, so I often make them whenever I feel like it. They are best enjoyed warm, as soon as they come out of the oven. Otherwise, store them in an airtight container for up to three to four days. They will harden a bit, but they are still good. Ensure that you follow this recipe precisely—the combination of wet and dry ingredients as well as the baking time produces the right texture of cookie, which is crunchy on the outside and soft and chewy on the inside.

Preheat oven to 350 °F (175 °C) and prepare a baking tray with parchment paper. Set aside the coarsely chopped almonds in a flat pan.

In a large bowl, whisk together the ground almonds, granulated sugar and icing sugar. Add the zest, almond extract and egg whites and mix together by hand or use a spatula until a firm paste is formed.

Take a scant tablespoon of the paste and roll it into a little cylinder about ¾ × 3 ½ inches (2 × 9 cm). Dip your fingers into some water if you find the dough needs a little more moisture to be easily rolled. Roll the cylinder in the coarsely chopped almonds, shape into a little crescent and place onto the baking pan. Make all cookies the same way. Bake for 15 minutes until the cookies are a very light golden brown.

Makes 25 cookies.

1 cup (250 mL) coarsely chopped hulled slivered almonds, for rolling in
2 ½ cups (625 mL) almond flour or ground hulled almonds
¾ cups (180 mL) granulated sugar
¼ cup (60 mL) icing sugar
zest of 1 large orange
1 tsp (5 mL) almond extract
2 large egg whites

EASTER BUTTER COOKIES (KOULOURAKIA)

Κουλουράκια

These butter cookies (or koulourakia) are traditionally made during Greek Orthodox Easter in Cyprus. They are crispy in texture and make a fantastic "dunking" cookie that is perfect to enjoy alongside tea or coffee. My mom makes them into delicate and beautiful little twist cookies. She has been doing this for years, so don't fret if yours don't look the same as the picture at first—it will come with practice.

Preheat oven to 350 °F (175 °C). Line a baking tray with parchment paper.

In a large bowl, beat the sugar and butter until fluffy. Add 4 egg yolks one at a time, beating well to incorporate. Add the vanilla powder.

In a separate, large bowl, mix the baking powder together with the flour. Slowly alternate adding the egg whites and the flour mixture into the butter mixture, using your hands to mix together the ingredients until a soft cookie dough is formed. You may need 3 ¾ cups (930 mL) all-purpose flour, or you may need up to 4 cups (1 L) to bring the dough together.

Take pieces of dough and shape them into ropes about ½ × 8 inches (1 × 20 cm). Fold the rope in half and twirl the ends together, creating a twist. Place the cookies on the baking tray and brush the tops with egg wash. Bake for about 25 to 27 minutes, until the cookies are golden brown.

Makes about 70 cookies.

1 cup (250 mL) sugar

1 cup (250 mL) unsalted butter

4 egg yolks (at room temperature) + extra 2 egg yolks, lightly beaten, for egg wash

½ tsp (2 mL) vanilla powder

4 tsp (20 mL) baking power

3 ¾ to 4 cups (930 to 1000 mL) all-purpose flour (approx.)

2 Tbsp (30 mL) vegetable shortening

4 egg whites (at room temperature), beaten until stiff peaks have formed

MARBLE CAKE (KEIK GEOGRAFIAS)

Κέικ Γεωγραφίας

This is a childhood favourite of mine. My aunt would always make this cake, ready to welcome us after our long trips from Canada, and I would wake up and eat it for breakfast on countless occasions. It's perfect with a cup of coffee or tea, and it's very easy to make.

3 ½ cups (875 mL) plain flour + extra for the pan

1 Tbsp (15 mL) baking powder

1 ½ cups (375 mL) sugar

4 oz (115 g) unsalted butter + extra for the pan

½ cup (125 mL) vegetable oil

5 eggs

¼ tsp (1 mL) pure vanilla powder

1 cup (250 mL) full fat milk

3 Tbsp (45 mL) cocoa powder

Preheat oven to 350 °F (175 °C). Butter and flour a Bundt pan that is 8 ½ inches (22 cm) in diameter.

Mix together the flour and baking powder. In another bowl, beat together the sugar, butter and oil until light and fluffy. Add the eggs to the liquid mixture one at a time, beating them in well. Add the vanilla to the liquid batter. Alternate adding the flour and milk to the batter, starting and ending with the flour.

Divide the batter in half. Add the cocoa powder to half of the batter. Alternate adding a scoop of the plain and a scoop of the chocolate batter into the bottom of the Bundt pan. Using a skewer, run it around the Bundt pan to create a marble pattern. Bake for 40 to 45 minutes, or until a skewer comes out clean.

Remove cake from the oven, let cool in the pan for 5 minutes, then remove the cake from the pan. Let cool before serving.

Makes 1 large Bundt cake (about 20 to 25 slices).

GRAPE JELLY (PALOUZES)

Ππαλουζἐς

Grape jelly (palouzes) is a traditional Cypriot sweet made in the fall during the grape harvest. The jelly has a distinctive jello-like texture and is sweet and creamy with a touch of vanilla or orange blossom taste that is best enjoyed while still warm. My aunt still makes a huge batch of it every fall to give to her friends and family, and the whole family comes together to help her make it. However, this is a recipe that less and less people make at home nowadays. It is also the first and most difficult step in making soutzoukos, a popular Cypriot snack consisting of threaded almonds dipped in palouzes and left to dry. I have included this recipe for preservation rather than for reproduction as it calls for an ingredient called Asprochoma, which translates to "white earth" and is literally a specific type of white chalky soil that can be found in the mountains in Cyprus. When added, it creates a chemical reaction that helps clear the cloudy grape juice and makes the jelly a touch sweeter. I know people who skip adding the Asprochoma or replace it with baking soda and still manage to make delicious grape jelly, but I have not tried this myself. If you would like to make this I would recommend making it with someone who has done it before as it can be a bit tricky.

3 ½ cups (875 mL) freshly squeezed Xynisteri grape juice (or juice from any white grape)
scant ¼ tsp (under 1 mL) white earth (Asprochoma)
2 ⅓ oz (70 g) traditional Cypriot "village flour" (or bread flour)
3 small rose-scented geranium leaves
½ tsp (2 mL) orange blossom water, divided
1 tsp (5 mL) water

Strain and pour the juice into a saucepan and bring to a boil. Skim off any froth that rises to the surface. Once the juice reaches a boil, add the Asprochoma. Boil for about 5 minutes, removing any foam that is created. Let the mixture cool for 10 minutes. The white earth will sink to the bottom of the juice.

Pour the juice into another saucepan, being careful not to also pour the white earth (which will be at the bottom of the pan). Pour 1 cup (250 mL) of this liquid into a bowl and add the flour. Whisk the flour mixture well until there are no clumps. Add the rose-scented geranium leaves to the saucepan.

Recipe continued...

Place the saucepan on the stove over medium heat. Once the juice begins to boil, remove the sweet-scented geranium leaves. Pour the flour mixture back into the saucepan through a strainer. Continue to whisk thoroughly as the liquid cooks. When the mixture begins to bubble again, add ¼ tsp (1 mL) orange blossom water. Continue to whisk the mixture. It is ready when it begins to have a glossy shine and many very small bubbles begin to appear, about 10 minutes from when the flour is added.

Sprinkle the remaining ¼ tsp (1 mL) orange blossom water and 1 tsp (5 mL) water into the bottom of a shallow glass serving dish. Pour the grape jelly into the dish. Eat while still warm, or store palouzes in the fridge for later.

Makes 2 large servings.

WALNUT SPOON
SWEETS (GLYKO KARIDAKI)

Γλυκό καρυδάκι

The word glyko literally translates to "sweet." Glyko is usually served alongside coffee, or after a meal. It can be made from a variety of fruits, vegetables or nuts (such as watermelon rind, figs, baby Seville oranges, baby eggplant, baby carrots, baby walnuts, bergamot rind or ground almonds), though the recipe changes depending on the fruit or vegetable. My favourite spoon sweet is walnut glyko, and I have included the recipe for that here. You can only make walnut glyko with young walnuts whose shells have not formed. You know the walnuts are okay to use if you are able to cut little triangles out from the top and bottom of the nut and can completely remove any shell that has started to form. The pickling lime powder is used to give the walnuts crunch—you need to be extremely careful with pickling lime powder and ensure that it is totally rinsed away. If you wish, simply omit the pickling lime powder, although this means your spoon sweets may not be as "crunchy."

Wearing gloves to protect your hands from the iodine in the walnut skin, use a kitchen peeler to peel off a layer from the green walnuts. Cut the tips off the walnuts in a triangle shape. Pierce each walnut through its vertical centre with a skewer. Place the walnuts in a bowl and cover with water. Leave for 7 days and change the water daily.

On the 7th day, change the water and add 1 cup (250 mL) of pickling lime powder to the water with the walnuts. Let rest for 4 hours. Thoroughly wash the walnuts with water to ensure that all the pickling lime powder has been completely rinsed away, then place the walnuts in a large pot of water.

Bring the pot of water with the walnuts to a boil for about 2 to 3 minutes. Empty the water and refill with cold water. Bring to a boil again. Empty the water. Add the juice of 4 lemons and as much water as needed to cover the walnuts. Leave for 1 hour. Empty the water.

Recipe continued...

50 fresh, young walnuts

1 cup (250 mL) pickling lime powder

4 ½ lemons, divided

4 ⅓ lb (2 kg) sugar

4 cups (1 L) water

1 Tbsp (15 mL) whole cloves

1 cinnamon stick

In another saucepan, add the sugar and about 4 cups (1 L) water. Heat the mixture on the stove until the sugar dissolves. Add the walnuts to the mixture and cook on medium heat for 7 minutes, allowing the mixture to foam. Let cool on the stove and cover with a lid.

For the next 3 days, bring the mixture to a boil for about 10 minutes, then let rest on the stove. On the 3rd day, add the cloves and cinnamon, boil and let the mixture reach its setting point (i.e., when the sugar syrup slowly drops off a spoon). During this last boil, also test to make sure that the walnuts are cooked. To do this, get a needle and pierce a walnut horizontally. Point the needle towards the ground and let the walnut try to slide off—if it does slide off, the walnut is cooked. Note that if you boil the mixture too much, the sugar syrup will begin to caramelize and you will need to add a little more water to make it more like syrup. When the setting point is almost reached, add the juice of ½ a lemon and turn off the heat. Let the mixture cool completely, then place the walnuts with syrup in sterilized jars.

Makes 50 walnut spoon sweets.

MERINGUE APPLE CAKE

I am not really sure why, but in Cyprus I find that a lot of desserts are made with meringue. This particular dessert was passed down to my mom from my nona (my godmother). It is a recipe that is really spectacular both in presentation and in taste, but it needs to be served immediately, otherwise the meringue will begin to melt. It will still taste good stored in the fridge one or two days after it is made, although the meringue will melt a little bit.

FILLING

6 to 7 apples, peeled and cut into thin slices (approx. 1 ¾ lb/785 g once cut and sliced)
½ cup (125 mL) sugar
2 Tbsp (30 mL) lemon juice
1 cinnamon stick
1 tsp (5 mL) butter

CAKE

½ cup (125 mL) unsalted butter (at room temperature) + extra for the pan
½ cup + 2 Tbsp (155 mL) sugar
4 egg yolks, reserve the whites for the meringue
1 tsp (5 mL) vanilla extract
1 cup (250 mL) all-purpose flour
1 tsp (5 mL) baking powder
3 Tbsp (45 mL) whipping cream

MERINGUE

4 egg whites (see above)
½ tsp (2 mL) fresh lemon juice
½ cup + 2 Tbsp (155 mL) sugar
½ tsp (2 mL) vanilla extract
½ cup (125 mL) slivered almonds

FILLING

Add the apples, sugar, lemon juice and cinnamon stick to a large pot and heat over medium until all the liquid evaporates. Stir the apples occasionally to ensure they are well-coated. Once the water has evaporated, add the butter and let cool.

CAKE

Preheat oven to 275 °F (135 °C). In a bowl, beat the butter with the sugar. Mix the egg yolks in one at a time, then add the vanilla extract. In a separate bowl, mix together the flour and baking powder. Alternate the flour mixture and whipping cream into the egg mixture, starting and ending with the flour. Butter and flour 2 springform pans that are about 9 ½ inches (24 cm) in diameter, and spread the batter evenly.

MERINGUE

Beat the egg whites with lemon juice to soft peaks. Add the sugar one teaspoon at a time, then slowly add the vanilla extract. Divide the meringue in half and spread one half over each cake batter. Spread the almonds overtop the meringues.

Bake the cakes (with meringues on top) for 45 minutes, until golden brown. Let cool slightly then remove from the pans to further cool. Once cooled, add the apple slices on top of one of the cakes and place the other cake on top of the apple layer. Serve immediately.

Makes 1 large double-tiered meringue cake (about 16 slices).

MOSAIC CAKE (DOUKISSA)

Δούκισσα

This is one of the first recipes I ever made. It is a cake that, although not very traditional, still very much reminds me of Cyprus. It can be found in many cafes and bakeries across Cyprus, and is often served as dessert at large family gatherings. The recipe is extremely simple, and the taste is comforting and indulgent. The recipe calls for a lot of butter, but this is necessary in order to help the cake set in the fridge.

Line a 4- × 12-inch (10 × 30 cm) loaf pan that is 3 inches (7 cm) deep with parchment paper. In a bowl, break the biscuits into small pieces and mix together with the roasted almonds. In another bowl, beat the eggs, egg whites, milk and brandy until mixed together.

In a glass bowl over a small pot of simmering water, melt the butter, sugar and milk chocolate. Ensure the bowl does not get too hot, otherwise the butter and milk chocolate will separate. Remove from heat and whisk in the drinking chocolate, cocoa powder and vanilla. Once mixed together, add the egg mixture, constantly whisking so that the eggs do not curdle. Place the bowl back over the pot of simmering water and continue to whisk until the eggs are cooked and the chocolate mixture is warm to the touch, about 5 minutes.

Pour the chocolate mixture over the cookie and nut mixture, ensuring it is well covered with chocolate. Scoop the cake batter into the loaf pan, pressing down on the ingredients to ensure the top of the cake is flat. Cover with plastic wrap and refrigerate for at least 5 hours or until set.

Turn over onto a serving plate, slice and serve.

Makes one 12-inch (30 cm) long loaf (about 20 to 25 slices).

¾ lb (350 g) Marie or tea biscuits

½ cup (125 mL) roasted slivered almonds

2 large eggs

3 large egg whites

5 Tbsp (75 mL) full fat milk

2 Tbsp (30 mL) brandy

1 ½ cups (375 mL) unsalted butter

¼ cup (60 mL) sugar

1 oz (25 g) milk chocolate

1 scant cup (just under 250 mL) drinking chocolate

¼ cup (60 mL) cocoa powder

¼ tsp (1 mL) vanilla powder

MOCHA POMEGRANATE BUNDT CAKE

Come autumn, pomegranates are everywhere. We have a tree at our village house, and it produces so many pomegranates that I often incorporate them into my baking. This is one of those recipes.

⅓ cup (80 mL) Cypriot coffee (or regular)
½ cup (125 mL) Greek yogurt
½ cup (125 mL) unsalted butter
¾ cup (180 mL) sugar
2 large eggs (at room temperature)
1 ¼ cups (310 mL) flour + extra for the pan
¼ tsp (1 mL) vanilla powder
½ cup (125 mL) cocoa powder
1 tsp (5 mL) baking soda
1 tsp (5 mL) baking powder
pinch of salt
1 Tbsp (15 mL) brandy
2 to 3 Tbsp (45 mL) strained fresh pomegranate juice
1 tsp (5 mL) milk (or more, if needed)
1 cup (250 mL) icing sugar

Prepare your coffee and let cool.

Grease and flour a Bundt pan approximately 8 ½ inches (22 cm) in diameter and preheat oven to 340 °F (170 °C). In a small bowl, mix together the coffee and yogurt. Beat the butter and sugar until creamy, then add the eggs one at a time, mixing them in well.

In a separate bowl, stir together the flour, vanilla powder, cocoa powder, baking soda, baking powder and salt. Alternate by adding the dry mixture and Greek yogurt mixture to the butter and sugar mixture. Start and end with the dry mixture. Pour the mixture into the Bundt pan and bake for about 30 to 35 minutes until a toothpick comes out clean. Remove from the oven and let cool for 10 minutes, then remove from the pan and let cool completely before frosting.

In a bowl, add the pomegranate juice and 1 tsp (5 mL) milk to the icing sugar until you reach a desired consistency. Drizzle the glaze overtop the cake and enjoy.

Makes 1 large Bundt cake (9 inches/22 cm in diameter, about 20 to 25 slices).

CHRISTMAS SHORTBREAD (KOURABIEDES)

Κουραμπιέδες

It is not Christmas in my family unless these cookies and melomakarona (p. 233) are made. I would describe these as Cypriot shortbread—they are buttery and nutty at the same time. I prefer mine extra nutty, for the added flavour.

1 cup (250 mL) butter
½ cup (125 mL) powdered sugar + extra for dusting
1 egg yolk
1 Tbsp (15 mL) brandy
¼ tsp (1 mL) vanilla powder
1 cup (250 mL) coarsely chopped, roasted hulled almonds
2 ⅔ cups (660 mL) all-purpose flour ¾ lb (360 g)

Preheat oven to 350 °F (175 °C). Beat the butter and powdered sugar together for 10 minutes, until light and fluffy. Continue to mix and add the egg yolk. When the egg yolk has been incorporated, add the brandy and vanilla. Continue to mix until well incorporated, about another 5 minutes. Stir the nuts into the mixture. Add the flour a little at a time, mixing the dough with your hand until the mixture holds together and does not stick. You may not need the last 2 Tbsp (30 mL) flour.

Roll out the dough with a rolling pin, about ½ inch (1 cm) thick. With a cookie cutter, cut out shapes from the dough. Place the cookies on a baking sheet.

Place the baking sheet in the oven for 20 to 22 minutes until cookies turn light brown. Remove the cookies from the oven and let them cool completely before generously dusting them with powdered sugar.

Makes about 25 cookies.

ORANGE BRANDY CAKE (VASILOPITA)

Βασιλόπιτα

Every New Year, people in Cyprus celebrate by making a vasilopita. A cross is made on top of the cake before it is sliced, and good luck in the year ahead is said to come to the person whose piece of cake has the hidden coin. There are many different versions of vasilopita, some of which have a lot of nuts in the cake itself or use nuts to decorate the top of the cake, spelling out the year to come or "happy new year" in Greek. If you wish to add some chopped nuts into the batter or on top to decorate the cake, you can do so. This is the cake I make every year, based off of my Aunt Myra's recipe. It is slightly sweeter than your typical vasilopita simply because I prefer it that way and often bring it as a dessert to dinner parties around Christmas and New Year. Also, I know this is a celebration cake, but I love it so much I usually make it more than once a year!

Preheat oven to 350 °F (175 °C). Grease and flour a 10-inch (25 cm) springform pan and line the bottom with parchment paper.

With a mixer, beat the butter and sugar well, about 10 minutes. Add the eggs one at a time, mixing them in well. Add the brandy and vanilla and mix until incorporated. Add the orange and lemon zests. (Don't worry if your batter begins to curdle at this stage.)

In a separate bowl, stir the baking powder and flour together. Add the orange juice and flour to the egg mixture, alternating with small amounts of each and starting and ending with flour. Pour the batter into the pan. If adding a coin into the cake, tightly wrap the coin in plastic wrap and drop it into the batter. Place in the oven for 60 minutes, until a toothpick inserted in the middle comes out clean.

Remove from the oven and let cool in the pan for 10 minutes. Remove from the pan and let cool on a cooling rack.

Makes 1 large cake (about 30 slices).

¾ cup (180 mL) unsalted butter

2 cups (500 mL) sugar

6 eggs

3 ½ Tbsp (52 mL) brandy

1 tsp (5 mL) vanilla

1 ½ Tbsp (22 mL) orange zest

½ Tbsp (7 mL) lemon zest

1 Tbsp (15 mL) baking powder

3 cups (750 mL) all-purpose flour

1 cup (250 mL) orange juice

CHOCOLATE STRAWBERRY TART

This is the first recipe that I made for my magazine recipe column in Cyprus, and also the first recipe and photograph of mine to grace a magazine's front cover. It is easy to make, and so decadent. It is perhaps one of my favourite desserts ever, and is always popular with dinner guests.

2 cups (500 mL) finely ground Oreo cookie crumbs (without the centre filling)
¼ cup (60 mL) melted unsalted butter
10 oz (285 g) excellent-quality semisweet chocolate, chopped into small pieces
1 ¼ cups (310 mL) whipping cream
1 Tbsp (15 mL) unsalted butter (at room temperature)
2 Tbsp (30 mL) brandy
5 to 8 fresh strawberries, quartered (optional)
¼ cup (60 mL) fresh blueberries (optional)
icing sugar, for dusting (optional)

Preheat oven to 375 °F (190 °C).

In a bowl, mix the cookie crumbs together with the melted butter. Press the cookie crust into the bottom and up the sides of an 8-inch (20 cm) tart pan with fluted sides and a removable bottom. Bake for 10 to 12 minutes. Let the tart base cool completely.

Place the chopped chocolate in a large glass bowl. Add the whipping cream to a small saucepan and bring to a bare simmer over a heated stove. Pour the heated whipping cream over the chocolate and gently stir with a spatula until the chocolate completely melts. Stir the softened butter and brandy into the chocolate mixture. Pour the chocolate mixture into the cooled tart. Refrigerate the tart for 5 hours or until set. Once the tart has set, decorate as preferred with strawberries, blueberries and/or icing sugar.

Makes 1 tart (8 inches/20 cm in diameter, about 12 slices).

POMEGRANATE PAVLOVA

I love making pavlovas with whatever fruits happen to be in season and a little fresh whipped cream. When I was writing this book, the pomegranates at my family's village house were in season—hence, this pomegranate pavlova.

MERINGUES

1 cup (250 mL) caster sugar, sifted

¼ tsp (1 mL) vanilla powder

1 tsp (5 mL) corn flour

4 egg whites

pinch of salt

1 tsp (5 mL) white vinegar

TOPPING

1 cup (250 mL) freshly squeezed
pomegranate juice

½ cup (125 mL) sugar

½ tsp (2 mL) lemon juice

1 ⅓ cups (330 mL) whipped cream

1 Tbsp (15 mL) icing sugar

pinch of vanilla

fresh pomegranate or other fresh
fruit (use as much as you wish)

Preheat oven to 235 °F (110 °C). Spread parchment paper on a baking tray.

MERINGUES

In a small bowl, mix together the caster sugar, vanilla powder and corn flour. In a bowl, add the egg whites and salt. Beat the egg whites until they become frothy, about 2 minutes. Add the vinegar and continue to beat the egg whites until medium peaks have formed. Begin adding the dry mixture one tablespoon at a time, mixing each tablespoon in well. Continue to beat the egg whites until they become thick and glossy and form stiff peaks.

Using a spatula, create a large circular meringue. Bake the meringue for 1 ½ hours. Do not open the oven door. After 1 ½ hours, turn off the heat, slightly open the oven door and let the meringue cool inside the oven.

TOPPING

Heat the pomegranate juice, sugar and lemon juice in a small saucepan over the stove. Cook and whisk the syrup until it has reduced by half and become thick. Before serving, beat the whipped cream with the icing sugar and vanilla in a small bowl. Top the meringue with the whipped cream, fresh pomegranate or other fresh fruit of your liking and a little syrup. Serve immediately.

Makes 1 pavlova (8 to 10 slices).

ROSEWATER FRANGIPANE PLUM TART

There is a region in Cyprus called Agros that is quite famous for its rosewater. I decided one year to try to incorporate it into a plum tart, as plums were also in season, and the result was this very stunning and absolutely delicious tart. The tart is glazed with rose jam, which you can usually find at a speciality Mediterranean or Middle Eastern grocery store. If you can't find rose jam, you can also use apricot jam or grape jelly as a glaze.

TART

In a little bowl, beat the egg yolk with the water.

In a large bowl, mix together all the dry ingredients. Add the butter and vegetable shortening to the dry ingredients and mix together with your fingers so that the mixture resembles little crumbs. Slowly add the egg and water mixture and use your fingers to mix the ingredients together until a dough begins to form.

Turn dough onto a floured surface and shape into a ball. Place the ball onto a large piece of plastic wrap, flatten it into a disk, wrap the disc in plastic wrap and place it in the fridge to chill for 1 hour.

Preheat oven to 375 °F (190 °C). Remove the dough from the fridge and roll out into a circle approximately ¼ inch (5 mm) thick. Place the dough into a tart tin with a removable bottom 9 inches (23 cm) across. Place the tart into the freezer for 20 minutes.

Remove tart from the freezer, place a piece of parchment paper covered in rice on top of the tart and bake for 20 minutes. Remove the parchment and rice and place the tart back into the oven, uncovered, for a further 5 minutes. Remove from the oven and let cool.

Recipe continued...

TART

1 large egg yolk

2 Tbsp (30 mL) cold water

¼ tsp (1 mL) vanilla powder

1 ½ cups (375 mL) all-purpose flour

2 Tbsp (30 mL) ground almonds

⅓ cup (80 mL) sugar

¼ tsp (1 mL) salt

2 ⅓ oz (70 g) unsalted cold butter

2 ½ Tbsp (37 mL) vegetable shortening
  (very cold)

FILLING

⅔ cups (160 mL) pistachio flour
  (2 ⅓ oz/70 g)

⅔ cups (160 mL) almond flour
  (2 ⅓ oz/70 g)

1 egg

1 tsp (5 mL) rosewater

2 Tbsp (30 mL) unsalted butter, melted

2 Tbsp (30 mL) brandy

2 red plums, pits removed, cut into
  thin slices

rose jam, lightly heated in a small
  saucepan, for glazing

FILLING

Mix together all filling ingredients except for the plums. Place the filling ingredients into the tart shell. Layer the plums next to each other (not overlapping) on top of the filling.

Place the tart back in the oven and bake for 30 minutes at 375 °F (190 °C), then turn down the temperature to 325 °F (160 °C) for a further 15 minutes. Cover with tinfoil if the tart appears to brown too much.

Remove and let cool. Once cooled, brush the plums with rose jam.

Makes 1 tart (about 12 slices).

COUSIN MARIA'S CAROB SHEET CAKE

I really feel that carob syrup is underrated. It's not just a chocolate substitute, and in fact doesn't taste at all like chocolate to me. To me it tastes more like toffee, caramel or even dates. In Canada, I often use it as a maple syrup substitute over pancakes. If you know how to use carob syrup, it can transform your dishes. Be sure to use the right-sized pan, as this cake contains no eggs and will struggle to rise in a smaller/deeper pan. This recipe was given to me by my cousin Maria, and will leave your kitchen smelling wonderful.

butter, for the baking dish
1 ½ cups (375 mL) carob syrup
½ cup (125 mL) water
1 cup (250 mL) coconut oil
1 cup (250 mL) orange juice
1 cup (250 mL) sugar
3 ½ cups (875 mL) all-purpose flour + extra for the baking dish
1 Ibsp (15 mL) baking powder
1 tsp (5 mL) baking soda
dash vanilla powder
¾ cup (180 mL) chopped walnuts, lightly toasted
icing sugar, for decoration (optional)

Preheat oven to 325 °F (160 °C). Butter and flour a 9- × 12 ½-inch (23 × 31 cm) baking dish that is 2 inches (5 cm) deep.

In a large bowl, mix the carob syrup and water together. Add the remaining wet ingredients and whisk together with the sugar until the sugar has dissolved.

In another bowl, mix together all the dry ingredients except for the walnuts and icing sugar. Slowly whisk the dry ingredients into the wet mixture. Once incorporated, add the walnuts and stir to incorporate. Pour evenly into the dish. Bake for 35 minutes, until a toothpick inserted into the centre comes out clean. Dust with icing sugar, if desired, and serve.

Makes 1 large flat sheet cake (about 24 pieces).

ROSE-SCENTED GERANIUM RICE PUDDING (RIZOGALO)

Ρυζόγαλο

Rose-scented geranium is a flower that you can find growing in the courtyards of most Cypriot houses. What I didn't realize until I grew up was that it is also used in traditional Cypriot dishes such as cherry spoon sweets, certain jams and grape jelly. Living in Cyprus, I began to use it in other recipes as well, such as this rice pudding. Traditionally, in my family, rice pudding was simply boiled rice and milk with a little cinnamon and honey on top. I was never a fan of this basic recipe, but with the addition of a few ingredients this dessert quickly became one of my favourites. A very refreshing, lovely dessert for the summer.

¾ cup (180 mL) short grain rice

1 ½ cups (375 mL) water + 2 Tbsp (30 mL) to dissolve cornstarch

4 cups (1 L) milk

¼ cup (60 mL) sugar

1 stick cinnamon

5 rose-scented geranium leaves

2 pieces orange peel (approx. ¾ × 2 ½ inches/2 × 6 cm)

1 tsp (5 mL) grated orange zest

1 ½ Tbsp (22 mL) cornstarch

ground cinnamon, for serving

honey, for serving

chopped pistachios, for sprinkling

Boil the rice in 1 ½ cups (375 mL) water until it has absorbed the water. Set aside.

Pour the milk into a pot and add the sugar, cinnamon stick, geranium leaves and orange peel. Bring the milk to a simmer. Once the milk is simmering, remove the geranium leaves, add the cooked rice and let it simmer for another 10 minutes.

Dissolve the cornstarch in 2 Tbsp (30 mL) water and add it to the pudding. Simmer the pudding for another 2 minutes. Remove the cinnamon stick and orange peel. Pour the pudding into little bowls. Cover the dishes with plastic wrap, let them cool and place them in the fridge for at least 5 hours, until the rice pudding has set. Serve with cinnamon, honey and chopped pistachios.

Makes 6 to 8 servings.

APRICOT JAM COOKIES (PASTA FLORA)
Πάστα Φλώρα

These little jam-filled cookies are made in Cyprus and Greece. The cookies are prepared in a pan sheet then sliced into little squares, and you can make them with different types of jam, although apricot jam is my favourite. It's funny, I don't see many people getting excited about these cookies in Cyprus, but whenever I make them abroad people absolutely think they are incredible. If you wish you can even serve them as a dessert—just leave them in the pan to cool, then cut and serve the cookies to your guests on the sheet pan itself.

Preheat oven to 360 °F (180 °C).

Beat the sugar with butter until fluffy. Add the egg yolks one at a time, beating them in well. Mix the baking soda with the lemon juice and add the lemon juice mixture, brandy and vanilla to the egg mixture. Mix in the flour and baking powder by hand, until a nice soft dough is formed (you may only need 3 cups/750 mL flour for this, or you may need a little bit more). The dough should not be sticky.

If using almond extract, mix together with the apricot jam.

Divide the dough in half. Press half the dough flat into the bottom of a 10- × 15-inch (25 × 38 cm) baking tray. Spread the jam on top (you may need a little more jam or a little less). Take the remaining dough and roll a long thin piece to place on top of the jam so that it follows the perimeter of the rectangular pan. Make more rolls and place them diagonally over the jam, in opposite directions, to create a diamond pattern. If you wish, place small roasted almond pieces in each diamond pattern.

Place in the oven and cook for about 35 to 40 minutes, until the dough is golden brown in colour. Remove from the oven and let cool. Once cool, cut into bite-sized squares.

Makes 50 to 54 cookies.

¾ cup (180 mL) sugar
1 cup (250 mL) unsalted butter
4 egg yolks
$\frac{1}{16}$ tsp (0.25 mL) baking soda
1 tsp (5 mL) lemon juice
2 Tbsp (30 mL) brandy
1 tsp (5 mL) vanilla extract
3 ½ cups (875 mL) all-purpose flour
1 tsp (5 mL) baking powder
1 ½ cups (375 mL) apricot jam
½ tsp (2 mL) almond extract (optional)
roasted almond pieces, for decoration

HONEY NUT COOKIES (MELOMAKARONA)
Μελομακάρονα

This is a strong contender for a lot of peoples' favourite Cypriot Christmas cookie. They are nutty and syrupy, with classic Christmas flavours of cinnamon, cloves and nutmeg. Interestingly, they also don't contain eggs. They have more of a crumbly and flaky texture than your typical Christmas cookie, with each bite filled with honey and spice flavour. I just adore these cookies, and couldn't wait for mom to finish baking them when we were little.

Preheat oven to 350 °F (175 °C)

COOKIES
Using a hand whisk, mix together all the cookie ingredients except for the flour, then slowly mix in the flour until the mixture becomes thick. Use your hands to finish mixing the dough. The dough is ready when it does not stick.

Form the cookies into oval shapes and place on a baking tray. Bake for 23 to 25 minutes. Remove from the oven and let cool completely.

SYRUP
Place all the syrup ingredients except the honey into a pot on the stove. Bring the syrup to a boil. Add the honey and bring to a boil again, then lower the temperature to a simmer.

Dip the cookies in the syrup a few at a time for 10 seconds each. Remove cookies and place them on parchment paper. Sprinkle with coarsely ground nuts.

Makes 30 to 40 cookies.

COOKIES
1 ½ cups (375 mL) vegetable oil

⅓ cup (80 mL) orange juice

2 tsp (10 mL) orange zest

⅓ cup (80 mL) icing sugar

1 tsp (5 mL) cinnamon

¼ tsp (1 mL) nutmeg

¼ tsp (1 mL) ground cloves

¾ tsp (4 mL) baking powder

¾ tsp (4 mL) baking soda

¼ tsp (1 mL) salt

¾ cup (180 mL) almond flour (lightly roasted optional)

3 cups (750 mL) all-purpose flour

SYRUP
1 cup (250 mL) water

1 cup (250 mL) sugar

1 Tbsp (15 mL) lemon juice

1 cinnamon stick

3 cloves

1 piece of orange rind (¾ × 4 inches/ 2 × 10 cm)

½ cup (125 mL) honey

½ cup (125 mL) ground roasted almonds, for sprinkling on top

½ cup (125 mL) ground roasted walnuts, for sprinkling on top

ONE-CUP SESAME ORANGE BISCOTTI (PAXIMADIA GLYKA)

Παξιμάδια γλυκά

My aunt always has a box of these cookies in her kitchen. They are so easy to make as it is essentially one cup each of all the main ingredients. The biscotti don't contain eggs or butter, as she typically makes them when she is fasting for religious reasons.

Preheat oven to 350 °F (175 °C). In a large bowl, whisk together the orange juice, sugar, vegetable oil and vanilla powder. Whisk in a bit of flour, baking powder and the almonds. Continue to whisk in the flour until a ball is formed, then switch to using your hands to mix the dough once it gets thick. The dough should be a bit sticky, but you should be able to roll it out when done. Keep adding 1 Tbsp (15 mL) of flour at a time until you get the desired consistency, but don't over-add the flour, as this will make your biscotti dense and in need of a longer baking time. The dough should be sticky but workable.

Cut the dough in half, roll it into logs about 12 inches (30 cm) in length. Roll the logs in sesame seeds and place on a baking sheet lined with parchment paper.

Using a serrated knife, cut diagonal slices just under ½ inch (1 cm) thick and about three-quarters of the way into the rolls. Bake for 30 minutes. Remove from the oven and slice all the way through, placing each slice of biscotti on its side and baking each side for another 5 to 10 minutes, ensuring they don't burn. Turn the oven off but let the biscotti dry out inside the oven for another 30 minutes.

Makes 32 to 40 biscotti.

1 cup (250 mL) freshly squeezed orange juice

1 cup (250 mL) sugar

1 cup (250 mL) vegetable oil

½ tsp (2 mL) vanilla powder

4 cups (1 L) flour (approx.)

1 Tbsp (15 mL) baking powder

1 cup (250 mL) chopped or slivered almonds

zest of 1 large orange

sesame seeds, for rolling in

CYPRIOT PEANUT AND SESAME BRITTLE (PASTELLI)

Παστελλάκι

I am constantly looking for good snack foods in Cyprus, and Cypriot pastelli is a fantastic sweet that I think is underrated. It is basically a Cypriot version of a crunchy nut bar. What I love about it is that it is so easy to make and lasts for a long time. In this version, I couldn't resist incorporating some chocolate into the recipe, but you can easily make it without. I have used carob syrup, but if you don't like the taste or don't have any on hand, you can simply add one more tablespoon of honey instead. Store the pastelli in an airtight container and it will last for a few weeks if properly stored. You will need a candy thermometer for this recipe in order to ensure the syrup is properly cooked.

1 ½ cups (375 mL) sesame seeds
1 ½ cups (375 mL) unsalted unroasted peanuts
vegetable oil, for oiling a surface
handful chocolate chips (optional)
1 cup (250 mL) white sugar
3 Tbsp (45 mL) honey
1 Tbsp (15 mL) carob syrup
2 Tbsp (30 mL) water

Roast the sesame seeds for 10 minutes and the peanuts for 20 minutes at 350 °F (175 °C). Let cool.

Drizzle a little vegetable oil overtop a slab of marble or onto a piece of parchment paper on a flat surface, which you will use to roll the sticky pastelli mixture onto later. Place a handful of chocolate chips onto the surface, if using.

In a small saucepan, add the sugar, honey, carob syrup and water. Place on medium-high heat and bring to a boil. Turn down the heat and simmer the syrup until it reaches 265 °F (130 °C) when measured with a candy thermometer. Add the nuts and seeds to the syrup in the saucepan and stir together until well-coated.

Dump the sticky mixture on top of the chocolate chips on the oiled work surface. Place a piece of oiled parchment paper on top of the pastelli, oiled side down. Using a rolling pin, roll the pastelli out into a thin slab. Remove the top piece of parchment paper. Using a large knife, slice the pastelli into thin strips. Let rest until ready to eat.

Makes a large bar of pastelli with as many pieces as you wish to divide it into.

AUNTIE MAROULLA'S PEACH AND ORANGE BLOSSOM TRIFLE (CHARLOTTA)

Σιαρλόττα

This autumn, my Thia Maroulla passed away. This was one of the recipes she handed down to me, so it is close to my heart. It is also a special recipe to me because in Canada we continue to use my great-aunt Athina's (who happens to be my Thia Maroulla's aunt) homemade orange blossom water in the custard. In every bite, I taste a little bit of Cyprus, and its flavours mix with my memories.

This dessert is very refreshing. It is served chilled and not overly sweet. I have called it a trifle, but when served the pieces come out easily, so it is not as messy as a trifle. I actually think of it as being halfway between a trifle and a Cypriot version of tiramisu. In Cyprus, it is known as a charlotta, and although many versions include diced Cypriot spoon sweets in the dessert, this particular recipe is simpler. I alternate between making this dessert in individual serving dishes and in one large Pyrex pan. Below, I have written the recipe for the pan. To make it in individual serving dishes, simply follow the recipe and use all the ingredients. This dish can last up to four days in the fridge and is best made a day ahead of when you are planning to serve it in order to let it set.

TRIFLE

one 28-oz (796 mL) can of peach halves in light syrup (approx. 7 halves, you may not need them all)

3 Tbsp (45 mL) brandy

1 ½ Tbsp (22 mL) roasted almond slivers + extra for decoration

1 pack of 24 ladyfingers (the type used to make tiramisu, you may not need them all)

Ingredients continued…

TRIFLE

Drain the peaches from the can and reserve the liquid (approx. 1 ⅓ cup/330 mL peach juice). Add the brandy to the liquid. Soak the ladyfingers in the liquid for about 3 seconds, until they have absorbed some of the liquid but are not soggy.

Place a layer of the ladyfingers in the bottom of a Pyrex pan that is about 12 inches (30 cm) long, 9 inches (23 cm) wide and 2 inches (5 cm) tall.

Thinly slice the peaches (each peach half yields about 6 to 8 slices). Add a layer of peaches above the ladyfingers. Sprinkle 1 ½ Tbsp (22 mL) roasted almond slivers on top of the sliced peaches.

Recipe continued…

CUSTARD

5 cups (1.25 L) milk, divided
⅓ cup (80 mL) sugar
7 ½ Tbsp (112 mL) cornstarch
½ Tbsp (7 mL) orange blossom water
⅛ tsp (0.5 mL) vanilla powder

WHIPPING CREAM

2 cups (500 mL) whipping cream
⅛ tsp (0.5 mL) vanilla powder
2 Tbsp (30 mL) icing sugar

CUSTARD

Dilute the cornstarch in 1 cup (250 mL) milk. Add the remaining 4 cups (1 L) milk and the sugar to a pot on the stove over just barely medium heat, whisking the mixture constantly. Once the mixture is hot to touch, add the cornstarch and milk mixture to the pot, continuously whisking the milk mixture until it thickens, becomes glossy and produces large bubbles. You can tell the custard is done when you dip a spoon in the custard and it comes out coated. Also, if you taste the custard it should taste like sweet milk, not cornstarch. Take the custard off the heat and whisk in the orange blossom water and vanilla powder.

Pour the custard over the peaches. Cover the top of the Pyrex pan with plastic wrap, leaving a corner uncovered so the heat can escape. Place in the fridge for at least 30 minutes. It is important to cover the custard with plastic wrap in order to ensure that no skin forms on the custard.

WHIPPING CREAM

Once the custard has set (about 5 hours), beat the whipping cream with a pinch of vanilla powder and 2 Tbsp (30 mL) icing sugar, until stiff.

SERVING

Remove the trifle from the fridge and add whipped cream on top. Decorate as you wish, with more roasted slivered almonds or leftover sliced peaches on top. Serve immediately or the next day. Store in the fridge.

Makes 15 to 20 servings.

CLEMENTINE'S CAKE (KALO PRAMA)

Καλὸν πρᾶμα

"Kalo prama" literally translates to "good thing." This is a popular dessert cake in Cyprus, and one that you can find in bakeries and on kitchen counters throughout the year. This recipe also has personal significance to me. I decided to create this recipe towards the end of the editing process. My first child, who we named Clementine (though not after the fruit), was born in January 2020. One of my favourite things to photograph while living in Cyprus were clementines and other citrus fruits, so coincidentally I had pictures of clementines dotted around our home even before the pregnancy. It seemed fitting that I include a recipe called Clementine's Cake.

This is one of my favourite desserts in Cyprus. It is easy to make, and best enjoyed during the months when citrus fruits are at their sweetest. It is a sweet cake and lasts only for a few days. I have used a traditional type of orange liquor that comes from Cyprus called "Filfar Orange Liqueur." If you cannot find it, simply substitute it with another type of orange liqueur or brandy if you wish. Also, feel free to use orange juice if you can't find fresh clementines.

CAKE

Grease a 9- to 10-inch (23 to 25 cm) diameter springform pan with butter and flour, and line the bottom with parchment paper. Preheat oven to 350 °F (175 °C).

Beat together the butter and berry sugar in a large bowl on medium-high speed for 5 minutes. Add the egg yolks one at a time, ensuring that each yolk is mixed in well before adding the next.

In a bowl, mix together the almond flour and semolina. With the mixer on low, alternate adding the almond flour mixture and clementine juice to the egg mixture, ending with the dry ingredients. Add in the clementine zest. The batter should become soft, but not really pourable.

In a separate bowl, whisk the egg whites until soft peaks form, then fold this into the batter. Add one large scoop first, using a spatula to mix it in and loosen the batter. Then, gently fold the rest of the egg whites into the batter until no egg whites remain.

Recipe continued...

CAKE

1 cup (250 mL) unsalted butter + extra for the pan

1 cup (250 mL) berry sugar

6 eggs, separated

1 ¾ cups (430 mL) almond flour + extra for the pan

½ cup (125 mL) extra fine semolina

zest of 6 clementines or 3 oranges

½ cup (125 mL) freshly squeezed clementine juice

SYRUP

½ cup (125 mL) granulated sugar

½ cup (125 mL) clementine juice

1 Tbsp (15 mL) lemon juice

3 Tbsp (45 mL) Filfar Orange Liqueur

Pour the batter into the pan and bake for about 50 minutes to 1 hour, until a skewer inserted into the cake comes out clean. You may need to cover the cake with tinfoil to prevent it from burning towards the end.

SYRUP

While the cake is baking, place the granulated sugar, clementine juice and lemon juice into a saucepan and bring to a boil. Simmer for 2 minutes, then remove from heat and stir in the Filfar Orange Liqueur.

Once you remove the cake from the oven, let it stand in the pan for 5 minutes.

Remove the cake from the pan and place it on a wire cooking rack over a large pan. Pierce the top of the cake all over with a toothpick. Spoon the syrup over the cake (both the cake and the syrup need to be warm). You may think the cake will not need all of the syrup, but don't be shy, it will absorb the liquid. Serve once cooled.

Makes 15 to 20 servings.

Suggested Menus

Many times in Canada people have asked me to cook them something "Cypriot," usually for dinner, but I have also offered to create a Cypriot breakfast on the odd occasion. At first I found the opportunity to cook something Cypriot both exciting and slightly overwhelming—I would find it difficult to narrow down just a few dishes to present to people to give them a true taste of Cyprus. Over the years, I have perfected my menus. There are so many options, so don't feel these are the only ones; however, these are the ones I find work for me and that are always enjoyed by my guests.

BREAKFAST

My typical breakfast in Cyprus consists of Greek coffee or a frappe together with some sort of breakfast pastry. We don't tend to have very large breakfasts in Cyprus, but there is usually a multitude of pastries to choose from in the morning. Some of my favourite breakfast items to choose between in Cyprus include a piece of toasted bread with local honey, tahini pies or perhaps some bulgur wheat pork pies that my aunt picked up on her trip to the local grocery store. When entertaining outside of Cyprus, I recommend serving Tahini Pies (p. 70) and either Halloumi Mint Scones (p. 60) or Traditional Sesame Bread Rings (p. 80), which can be served alongside some fresh or grilled/fried slices of halloumi, good-quality honey, butter and mosphilo jelly or another type of jam.

The Tahini Pies will take some preparation the day before, but this is such a classic favourite breakfast item in Cyprus and worth sharing with those unfamiliar with Cypriot cuisine. They can simply be enjoyed on their own, without any accompaniments. The Halloumi Mint Scones can be made the morning of entertaining and are easy to make. They are fantastic warm, and showcase the traditional Cypriot flavour combination of halloumi and mint. I sometimes enjoy putting butter and jam on top of the scones, which creates a delicious salt and sweet flavour combination. Traditional Breakfast Sesame Bread Rings will also take some preparation the day before. If you have any mosphilo jelly on hand, it is wonderful to enjoy over the warm scones or on the sesame bread rings. If you do not, simply use any other kind of sweet jam—it will pair well with the bread rings or scones.

Lastly, if you have the time, I would recommend making Bulgur Wheat Pork Rolls (p. 77)—which are one of my favourite savoury breakfast items back home—or serving some Spinach Pies (p. 56). Spanakopites can be made ahead of time, which is always useful when planning.

- ❖ Tahini Pies (p. 70)
- ❖ Spinach Pies (p. 56)
- ❖ Bulgur Wheat Pork Rolls (p. 77)
- ❖ Halloumi Mint Scones (p. 60)
- ❖ Traditional Sesame Bread Rings (p. 80)
- ❖ Mediterranean Medlar Jam (p. 179)
- ❖ Cypriot Coffee (p. 24) or Frappe (p. 35)

DINNER FOR TWO

If I am cooking for two, I like to keep things simple and I try to recreate what I would typically eat in Cyprus at home. Nothing fancy, but I still aim to showcase the delicious flavours that can be found. I will usually start by offering a small starter, such as Spinach Pies (p. 56) or Olive Bread (p. 40) that I have already made and simply reheat from the freezer.

If I am pressed for time when preparing a main course I will make either Cypriot Lentils (p. 155) to serve alongside some good-quality feta cheese and/or Greek yogurt, or the Lamb Orzo Stew (p. 164). These dishes are two of the easier ones to make, and they don't compromise on flavour at all. I pair them with Cypriot Potato Salad (p. 92) or Tomato and Feta Salad (p. 89).

If I have more time, I will usually aim to showcase a classic home-cooked Cypriot meal, and make Pork Meatballs (p. 156) with Tomato Bulgur Wheat Pilaf (p. 107), which can be served alongside good-quality Greek yogurt and Cypriot Potato Salad (p. 92) or Tomato and Feta Salad (p. 89). The Zucchini Patties (p. 159) are a very good option for vegetarians.

For dessert, I will make the Orange Brandy Cake (p. 217), as it is enjoyed tremendously and lasts for a few days if not entirely eaten. Another option I sometimes choose is to simply make the Apricot Jam Cookies (p. 231), as they taste a bit like a jam tart and last for days. Guests usually enjoy taking some home with them too!

- ❖ Spinach Pies (p. 56)
- ❖ Olive Bread (p. 40)
- ❖ Cypriot Lentils (p. 155) if I am cooking for vegetarians, or Lamb Orzo Stew (p. 164) if pressed for time
- ❖ Zucchini Patties (p. 159) if I am cooking for vegetarians, or Pork Meatballs (p. 156) if not, both with Tomato Bulgur Wheat Pilaf (p. 107) if there is time to prepare
- ❖ Cypriot Potato Salad (p. 92) or Tomato and Feta Salad (p. 89)
- ❖ Cypriot Coffee (p. 24)
- ❖ Orange Brandy Cake (p. 217)
- ❖ Apricot Jam Cookies (p. 231)

DINNER FOR SIX TO EIGHT

Every large family gathering in Cyprus has two items that make an appearance: Stuffed Vegetables (p. 141) and Cypriot Lasagna (p. 144). For this reason, I always make sure to include these two dishes when cooking for four or more people in North America as well. One is vegetarian, and one is meat-based, allowing me to be able to offer both a meat and vegetarian option to guests.

To start, I usually put out some Spinach Pies (p. 56), and I buy some pita bread and serve it with either Tahini–Garlic Dip (p. 180) or Cucumber, Garlic and Mint Dip (p. 174). I will also put out some fresh or grilled slices of halloumi, Coriander Smashed Olives (p. 176) or Pickled Caper Shoots (p. 171) if I have any on hand (otherwise I may just buy some good-quality kalamata olives from the store).

I always ensure I have a salad as well, and I find that a Tomato and Feta Salad (p. 89) is always welcome whether it's summer or winter (and it's easy to make).

Lastly, for dessert, I usually make Mrs. Popi's Pistachio Baklava (p. 188), which is always a crowd-pleaser and can be made a couple days in advance. I serve it with Cypriot Coffee (p. 24), for anyone who wishes to try the same. I also find that Clementine's Cake (p. 243) is a favourite with dinner guests, as well as Auntie Maroulla's Peach and Orange Blossom Trifle (p. 238) in the summertime. Also, if I have any already-made walnut spoon sweets in the cupboard I will offer them with the coffee.

- Spinach Pies (p. 56)
- Tahini–Garlic Dip (p. 180)
- Cucumber, Garlic and Mint Dip (p. 174)
- Coriander Smashed Olives (p. 176) or store-bought kalamata olives
- Pickled Caper Shoots (p. 171)
- Halloumi (p. 109), sliced (serve fresh or grilled)
- Tomato and Feta Salad (p. 89)
- Cypriot Lasagna (p. 144)
- Stuffed Vegetables (p. 141)
- Mrs. Popi's Pistachio Baklava (p. 188), Clementine's Cake (p. 243) or Auntie Maroulla's Peach and Orange Blossom Trifle (p. 238)
- Walnut Spoon Sweet (p. 203)
- Cypriot Coffee (p. 24)

Cyprus Markets

One thing I love about Cyprus is the homegrown vegetables and fruits, and when I'm in Cyprus I will often wake up very early and head off to the markets in search of whatever I need. Visiting a Cypriot market is an experience. They are not particularly picturesque or relaxing. In fact they are often chaotic, with makeshift setups that are busy, loud and often hot, and are usually packed with shoppers searching for the best produce at the best price. And I absolutely love it. In my opinion, these markets are still some of the best places to find the freshest seasonal fruits and vegetables at a cheap price. They are also filled with other traditional goodies: homemade halloumi, nuts, eggs, freshly made bread.

Strangely, from what I have observed, the old municipal markets located in town centres that used to be very busy in the past are not as busy anymore, nor do they have the large selections they used to, even though the buildings themselves are still beautiful and it can be more relaxing to browse there. Instead, I have found that localized markets are becoming increasingly popular, although it can be difficult to know where and when these markets will occur. For this reason, while I have included some tips for attending the markets, I have omitted to mention where and when these markets occur. The best way to find this out is to ask a local where and when the markets are.

Given their importance to me, as well as how challenging I have found the process of tracking down these markets to be, I thought I would share a little information in case anyone wishes to visit one. Please note that locations and times may occasionally change, but I hope that this information will at least provide a start to anyone visiting or living in Cyprus who wants to explore the local markets.

A Few Tips

❖ Make sure to go early, as a lot of produce will be sold early, and in the summertime the heat becomes unbearable after about 10 a.m.

❖ Don't be afraid to browse around, as even within the market there will be different qualities of the same produce sold at varying prices.

❖ Don't be afraid to ask questions about where the produce came from or how old it is—usually vendors will let you sample the produce, too, so don't be shy.

❖ If you are planning to buy a lot, remember that only plastic carrier bags are provided, so you may have to walk back and forth to your car a few times.

❖ Bring cash with you to the markets, as vendors do not take cards.

It also bears mentioning that there are quite a few smaller grocery stores in Cyprus that carry fresh produce, as well as an assortment of honeys, cheeses, olives and other locally made products. I would definitely recommend a visit to one of these grocery stores if you are interested in buying locally made products. They also tend to be cheaper than the larger grocery chains. With the above in mind, here is a list of my top three favourite markets in Cyprus. Please do note that this list is not exhaustive, these are just my favourites, where I often go myself.

LIMASSOL

Organic Farmers' Market

Ovidiou Street, Ayia Fyla, 3112 Limassol
Saturdays: 9:00 a.m. to 1:00 p.m.
Sells: fruits, vegetables, fresh eggs, rabbit, homemade
organic cheeses, milk, homemade tomato sauces.

This is the only certified organic farmers' market I
know of on Cyprus, and I love it. The tomatoes are
exceptional. Chrystalla is very kind and usually
has a complimentary sample of her baked goods
on offer for those who visit. Go early because it is
extremely popular.

Kato Polemidia Market

Aigisthou Road, Kato Polemidia
Wednesdays and Sundays: 7:30 a.m. to 12:00 p.m.
Sells: fruits, vegetables, flowers, traditional breads, traditional dried
meats, pulses, Cyprus sweets.

Though this is not a pretty market, it is a busy market frequented by
many locals. The prices are great and the produce is very fresh. There
is a makeshift coffee shop, and the vendors are very friendly. Keep an
eye out for the freshly made bread, it is excellent!

NICOSIA

Oxi Square Market

Oxi Roundabout, Constantine Paleologou Street, Nicosia
Wednesdays and Saturdays: 6:00 a.m. to 1:00 p.m.
Sells: fruits, vegetables, traditional dried meats, pulses, olives, flowers,
traditional Cypriot bread.

This is a chaotic city market, but it has one of the largest selections of
fruits, vegetables, nuts, cheeses, plants and more. It often sells foods
that I cannot find in the big grocery stores, but that I know are in season.

259

Acknowledgments

To my Dad, who made everything possible. To my mom, who is the best cook I know. This book should really have your name on the front cover as well, it is as much your accomplishment as it is mine.

To my aunties Evri, Kalo, Maroulla and Myra, whose love I don't know what I would have done without all these years and whose traditional recipes I hope I have done justice to. Thank you for finally giving in and letting me use the measuring cups!

To my sister Stephanie.

To my family: my love, Steven Doyle, thank you for your incredible support and advice and for being an absolute sweetheart. I love the fact that you love food as much as I do, possibly more! And to Clementine, who is soundly sleeping in her bassinet as I type this sentence.

To Alexandra Phylaktis.

To my dear friends and family who believed I could, and who supported me with their encouragement, help and advice, even when the blog did not exist. In particular: Alexis Kallis, Amelie Pavlou Michaelides, Arthur Marriott QC, Athos Kasinos, Chryso Lefou, David Lewis, Dr. Economides, Elena Ivanova, Eleni Kasapi, Fiona Taylor, Haruka Sakaguchi, Ilias Koumbaris, Jessica Cherniak, Ju-lie Loucas, Kim Wheddon, Loucas Kyriakides, Marilou Christodoulides, Nancy Murphy, Nicolas Iordanou, Nona Kallis, Paola Papacosta, Petros Petrou, Rachel Chyrsostom, Rachel Lewis, Ravneeta Roy, Rhea Frangofinou, Dr. Savvas Frangos, Tammy Loucas, Terri Zakus, Thia Maroulla, Tina Petropolous, Uncle Gabriel and Uncle John.

To Dr. Cecilia D'Felice, for giving me hope and literally helping me find my voice.

To Ernie the pug, for cleaning the kitchen floor so I don't have to.

Professionally, to Benedetta and Emanuelle Tosi, for taking an interest in publishing my book and making it

a reality, to Mara Pellegrini for reading my blog in the first place and to Sharon Fitzhenry and Holly Doll at Fitzhenry & Whiteside for making this beautiful English edition. To Patrick Geraghty and Tanya Montini for your incredible help with this project, answering all of my questions and making this book so beautiful and easy to read. To Lia Crowe for the beautiful portraits of me and my family on pages vi and 265. To my first clients for believing in me from the beginning: Mitsides and Foodsaver Stores.

To George of Lemba Pottery, who makes the most beautiful ceramics in Cyprus, which can be seen dotted around in the pages of this book. I highly encourage anyone visiting Cyprus to visit his workshop in Lemba.

To everyone who read the blog and supported me with your kind words along the way, as well as to all those I have connected with on Instagram, who are proof that sometimes you do not have to meet in person to forge a friendship. Thank you so, so much. This book would not exist without you.

About the Author

Christina Loucas is a recipe developer, photographer, food stylist and creator of the popular food blog Afrodite's Kitchen.

She was raised on Vancouver Island, Canada, by Greek–Cypriot parents. Her love of food and cooking is a byproduct of having grown up surrounded by fantastic food—her dad was an award winning restaurateur, and her mother an accomplished baker.

She has a degree in Jurisprudence from Oxford University and a BSc in Government and Economics from the London School of Economics. She worked for six years as an international arbitration lawyer in London, England before deciding to move to Cyprus.

During her move to Cyprus, she started the food blog Afrodite's Kitchen in order to try to preserve traditional Cypriot recipes she thought were being forgotten. She now writes recipes and photographs food for a variety of clients while continuing to post recipes on her blog.

She enjoys shopping at farmers' markets in Cyprus, visiting her mother's village in the Cypriot countryside, cooking with her mother and generally making a mess in her kitchen and growing her mismatched collection of kitchenware and cookbooks.

She is currently based in Victoria, British Columbia, Canada, with her always-hungry pug Ernie and her partner Steve, as well as her newly born little sous-chef Clementine. She can be found on a day-to-day basis on Instagram at @afroditeskitchen cooking up traditional and modern Cypriot recipes. This is her first cookbook in North America. She has previously published in Germany and Italy.

Index

271